IMAGES OF THE
NATIONAL ARCHIVES

SUFFRAGETTES

IMAGES OF THE NATIONAL ARCHIVES

SUFFRAGETTES

LAUREN WILLMOTT

PEN & SWORD
HISTORY

AN IMPRINT OF PEN & SWORD BOOKS LTD.
YORKSHIRE ~ PHILADELPHIA

First published in Great Britain in 2018 by
Pen & Sword History
An imprint of
Pen & Sword Books Ltd
Yorkshire - Philadelphia

The National Archives is the official archives and publisher for the UK Government, and for England and Wales. We work to bring together and secure the future of the public record, both digital and physical, for future generations.

The National Archives is open to all, offering a range of activities and spaces to enjoy, as well as our reading rooms for research. Many of our most popular records are also available online.

Typeset in Minion Pro 11/14.5 by
Aura Technology and Software Services, India

Printed and bound in India by Replika Press Pvt. Ltd.

Pen & Sword Books Ltd incorporates the Imprints of Pen & Sword Books Archaeology, Atlas, Aviation, Battleground, Discovery, Family History, History, Maritime, Military, Naval, Politics, Railways, Select, Transport, True Crime, Fiction, Frontline Books, Leo Cooper, Praetorian Press, Seaforth Publishing, Wharncliffe and White Owl.

For a complete list of Pen & Sword titles please contact

PEN & SWORD BOOKS LIMITED
47 Church Street, Barnsley, South Yorkshire, S70 2AS, England
E-mail: enquiries@pen-and-sword.co.uk
Website: www.pen-and-sword.co.uk

or

PEN AND SWORD BOOKS
1950 Lawrence Rd, Havertown, PA 19083, USA
E-mail: Uspen-and-sword@casematepublishers.com

CONTENTS

Glossary 6

Key Suffrage Societies 6

Introduction 7

Chapter 1:   The 'Woman Question', 1867–1903 9
Chapter 2:   The Birth of the Suffragette, 1903–1913 14
Chapter 3:   More Deeds, Less Words, 1913–1914 50
Chapter 4:   Rising Frustrations in other Suffrage Organisations 81
Chapter 5:   A New War 86
Conclusion: New Feminism and Legacy 94

GLOSSARY

Suffrage – the right to vote in political elections.
Suffragists – an advocate of extending voting rights to women. It can include both militant and non-militant activists.
Suffragettes – women seeking the vote through militant methods.

KEY SUFFRAGE SOCIETIES

Actresses' Franchise League (AFL)
East London Federation of Suffragettes (ELFS)
Men's Committee for Justice to Women
Men's League for Women's Suffrage
National Union of Women's Suffrage Societies (NUWSS)
New Constitutional Society for Women's Suffrage
Suffrage Vigilance League
Women's Freedom League (WFL)
Women's Political and Social Union (WSPU)
Women's Tax Resistance League

INTRODUCTION

On 20 June 1837, Princess Alexandrina Victoria was pronounced Queen Victoria of Britain. With an annual income of £385,000 (the equivalent of approximately £17 million today) and an Empire that soon encompassed one-fifth of the world's population, she became the richest and most powerful woman not only in Britain, but in the world.

Elsewhere in Britain, married women were not even able to own property, let alone an Empire, nor were respectable women expected to work. A woman's place, as dictated by the patriarchal ruling of Victorian Britain, was in the home, nurturing a family. Respectable men, on the other hand, were the 'breadwinners', the providers and protectors of the family. Despite the young Queen heading the government, she was considered a temporary anomaly; with her male advisors, male MPs and male Prime Minister – as voted for by a small number of men – politics remained, very much, a man's world.

Yet, some women were not content to remain in these distinct and prescribed spheres. One by one, the restrictions imposed on them were gradually challenged. Sometimes this was by lone individuals, such as Caroline Norton who demanded, successfully, custody of her children after her husband absconded with them. More often, though, these challenges were raised by small women-only organisations and committees, which were springing up across the country, campaigning to overturn specific issues. In 1859, the Society for Promoting Women's Employment was established, followed by the Married Women's Property Committee. The Ladies' National Association for the Repeal of the Contagious Diseases Act was founded, led by Josephine Butler. The Association campaigned to overturn the double standards of the Contagious Diseases Act of 1864, which aimed to check venereal disease in the army by arresting and examining prostitutes only. It took twenty years of campaigning before the act was finally repealed in 1886.

Perhaps, though, the most iconic element of this emerging Victorian feminism was the struggle for the vote. The first claim for women's votes came in response to the expansion of male suffrage in 1867 for more working-class men than ever before. If they can vote, some women began to ask, why can't we? John Stuart Mill's bold suggestion to change 'man' to 'person' in amendments to the Reform Act was thoroughly quashed by an overwhelming majority of MPs. This setback, however, did not deter Lydia Becker, Millicent Fawcett and hundreds of others, who were about to embark upon a fifty-year arduous journey to transform women's lives.

To do this, they demanded the vote, a say in the political arena to enable moral, social and cultural improvements for women. With this, women's suffragism was born.

Throughout this book, we will delve into the world of suffrage. Using documents and images from The National Archives, we will trace this journey, and gain a unique insight into the trials, tribulations and turmoil of the suffrage struggle. The story of the Pankhursts' headstrong leadership and the dramatic Derby Day death of Emily Wilding Davison has become embedded in popular consciousness, but the story of suffragism is much bigger than a few fervent militants. We will follow the story of thousands of individual women (and men), in dozens of organisations across the nation, each of whom contributed to the long fight against patriarchal rule and oppression - and how they were ultimately able to emerge victorious.

CHAPTER 1

THE 'WOMAN QUESTION', 1867–1903

The Victorian era sees huge changes: railways are rapidly criss-crossing Britain, London becomes home to the world's first underground tube in 1863, and there is a population rise to match the dizzying growth of industrialisation. Amidst this progressive momentum, new ideas are springing up that challenge the norms. In 1848, millions of working class Chartists call for universal manhood suffrage; Charles Darwin's 1858 theory of evolution initially shakes prevalent Christian beliefs centred on creationism;, and democratic values are becoming high on the Liberal agenda in particular;.

Amongst those challenging the status quo are a smattering of middle and upper-class women aggrieved by specific injustices. Some of these women recognise the power of the collective. They come together and form a female committee to gather support for the Married Women's Property Bill – a bill that would allow women the right to keep their earnings after marriage. Although the group, the first of its kind, muster around 26,000 signatures in support of it, the bill is nevertheless defeated. In spite of – or perhaps because of – the failure of the group's first attempt to lobby for change, the committee has given some of these women a taste for protest.

The Langham Place Group is formed. As middle-class women with few opportunities to hone their own intellectual ambition, they focus on a vision for improved opportunities for women in education and employment in wider Victorian Britain. Some of these women, not content with voicing ideas for change within their own group, attend the Kensington Ladies Discussion Society, a space for like-minded, intelligent and ambitious women to voice ideas to address women's inequalities. It is here that, once again, the issue of female suffrage is raised.

In 1866, inspired by a reading of the Reform Act, which will extend voting rights to more men than ever before, members of the Kensington Ladies' Discussion Society, including Barabara Bodichon and Elizabeth Garrett, decide the time is right for parliament to hear of demands for the vote of all householders – "regardless of sex". A petition is hurriedly drafted, and within the

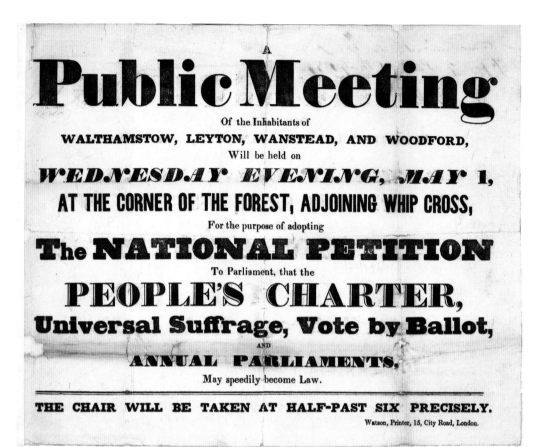

A notice for a public meeting being held in East London on the issue of universal male suffrage. Between 1837 – 1848, 'Chartists' campaigned for universal male suffrage, voting by ballot and for annual Parliaments. *EXT 3/36*

month nearly 1,500 women throughout the country have signed. Their demands are presented to parliament by John Stuart Mill, a sympathetic, radical, Liberal MP. It is rejected, but the seeds of female empowerment via enfranchisement have been well and truly sown. Spurred on by this set-back, a National Society for Women's Suffrage is founded within the year.

Hundreds of women's suffrage groups spring up across the country, and are particularly strong in London, Manchester and Edinburgh. Eventually, a Central Committee of the National Society for Women's Suffrage is formed in Manchester. Millicent Fawcett, just one of hundreds of women growing impatient with the lack of progress so far, joins this Committee, optimistic that a centralised group will increase pressure on parliament and force change through. Her natural leadership, passion and reason does not go unnoticed and she soon becomes a prominent figure within the Committee.

Women's demands for increased rights threaten the status quo of Victorian Britain and the 'natural' roles of men and women. The 'New Woman' begins to appear in literature and art from 1894 onwards and characteristically questions the institution of marriage, and the idea of a woman as a 'sexless' being. Instead, she is independent, educated, ambitious and less prudish than the 'ideal' domesticated, subservient and dependent Victorian woman. To advocates of women's rights, the 'New Woman' is emancipated.

To opponents of women's rights, she is cause for alarm. Expressions of incredulity, masking, in part, a fear of change, can be found in cartoons, postcards and even toys. On this toy, copyrighted in 1901, the 'New Woman' is wearing manly attire – trousers, a shirt and a tie. For feminists, these 'rational' clothes demonstrate an objection to the physical restrictions of 'proper' female clothes – corsets, hoop skirts and dresses. To opponents of feminism, cross-dressing, outside of entertainment halls and concerts, is closely associated with lesbianism; she is therefore to be considered a moral degenerate. The cigarette is symbolic of her emancipation, yet this is at the expense of her 'natural' maternal and domestic instincts as shown by the two crying babies directly above her. The, quite literally, broken man reflects the fears of what this means to men;

The 'New Woman' is depicted in books, artwork and newspapers. This 'New Woman Toy' from 1901 depicts the 'New Woman' as manly. Many feared that the 'New Woman' represented a threat to the Victorian feminine ideal. *COPY 1/174/312*

after all, by questioning the natural role of women, the 'New Woman' is opposing the natural role of men as protectors, providers and 'masters' of women. To reassert the 'natural' order, this toy packaging makes sure to point out that the 'New Woman' is doomed.

In the minds of opponents, she represents a moral, cultural and societal decay. Opponents refuse to believe that a woman can choose not to marry and to live an independent life. Instead, they argue, she wants to marry but cannot find a husband; her 'emancipation' is nothing but a façade to hide her failures as a woman. The New Woman, they argue, is a Wrong Woman.

More importantly, this image is often projected onto suffragists – by the 1890s termed feminists. It is an image that opponents of suffrage will repeatedly revert to over the coming years: feminism as sexual degeneracy, lesbianism and manliness. Quite simply, suffragism is outrageous.

The year 1897 sees Queen Victoria's Diamond Jubilee celebration. To the women, this year – the year that the nation is celebrating a *woman* becoming Britain's longest ever reigning monarch - would present the perfect opportunity for female enfranchisement to be enacted.

The mood of the nation, and across the Empire, is joyous. A bank holiday is declared, and festivals occur in many towns and cities. Suffragists themselves are also feeling almost victorious; less than a year earlier they had successfully presented a petition containing over 257,000 names to parliament in support of the vote, and a vote for a second reading of a bill, presented by Ferdinand Faithfull Begg, gained a majority in February.

Like hundreds of local governments, schools, and cultural, religious and political societies nationwide, Millicent Fawcett, on behalf of the Combined Committees of National Society for Women's Suffrage, sends Queen Victoria a formal congratulatory address.

In the address, the Combined Committee – representing various women's suffrage societies - believe this year is an event 'specially memorable for the women' of Britain and its Empire. They do not mention suffrage demands, or Victoria's previous scorn of their demands (Victoria, in fact, had previously noted in her diary that the business of Women's Rights is 'mad wicked folly' whose supporters 'ought to get a good whipping.') Instead, Millicent Fawcett, joins in the spirit of congratulations and joy, and instead offer thanks to Victoria for the rights women have gained throughout her reign. Despite remaining inequalities, women have achieved considerable success: the first women are permitted to attend Cambridge University (although not to receive degrees); the Married Women's Property Act has been passed, entitling women to keep their property after marriage; and women have even been granted the vote in the Isle of Man in 1881. Along the edges of this elaborately decorated address, the gains made by women in the arts and science; domesticity; charity; industry; and education, are portrayed.

Despite this, the women's suffrage movements, aware of the negative connotations of the 'New Woman', choose to portray Victoria first and foremost as a mother – a mother of her people. They are aware that motherhood remains central to the idea of femininity but – as with Victoria – they hope it is a role that can be combined with active participation in the political sphere. The moral, nurturing and caring virtues associated with motherhood – epitomised by the portrayal of Queen Victoria surrounded by children - can only serve to advance and improve society, as Victoria has in her reign.

However, the optimism of the women's movement does not last long. The second reading of Faithfull Begg's bill is never discussed in parliament. This defeat, despite the hope portrayed in this address and the formation of the National Union for Women's Suffrage Society (NUWSS) just a few months later, causes a temporary lull in the female suffrage movement.

Hundreds of societies and organisations send congratulatory addresses to Queen Victoria on her Diamond Jubilee in 1897. This one is sent by Millicent Fawcett on behalf of the National Society for Women's Suffrage. *PP1/349/2*

CHAPTER 2

THE BIRTH OF THE SUFFRAGETTE, 1903-1913

Despite the period of relative calm, suffrage groups, particularly in the North of England, are quietly continuing to mobilise support. In 1901, the Lancashire Women's Textile Workers group rally over 33,000 working-class women to sign a petition in support of female suffrage. Parliament ignores their demands. The traditional, constitutional method of petition, so valued by reformers and social activists throughout British history, is achieving little to further women's rights.

Signs of discontent are beginning to emerge, spurred on by the advances of women's suffrage elsewhere in the British Empire and its former colonies. New Zealand had granted women the vote in 1893, and most states in Australia had followed suit by 1902.

Emmeline Pankhurst, a staunch supporter of the women's movement, cannot hide her frustrations with the NUWSS' lack of progress to date. With her daughters, Sylvia, Christabel and Adela, she forms a breakaway group in Manchester, the Women's Labour Representation Committee. Swayed by her own socialist beliefs, it is initially a pressure group within the Independent Labour Party, a new political party that fights for the rights of the working class. This group soon becomes the Women's Social and Political Union (WSPU).

Since petitions are not achieving the desired results, the WSPU know that they must find a new way to put women's suffrage at the forefront of politician's minds and convince them of its necessity. From 1903 to 1905, they are no more than a peripheral group with only a handful of members, holding meetings at the Pankhursts' Manchester home. But, with a new strategy of "Deeds not Words", this is about to change.

The heckling of politicians becomes a trademark of the WSPU in its early years. Winston Churchill, a new Liberal MP, is one of the first to experience persistent interruptions and jeering by WSPU members. But he is certainly not the last.

With an election on the horizon in 1905, political meetings are everywhere; the WSPU are almost spoilt for choice over which ministers to heckle. Annie Kenney, a mill worker from Oldham, Lancashire and one of the only working-class figures to hold a senior position in the movement - and Christabel Pankhurst, sit quietly at a Liberal Party meeting in Manchester Free Trade Hall, led by the Foreign Secretary, Sir Edward Grey, waiting for the opportune chance to strike. The moment comes during question time. They obstinately demand to know if a Liberal government would support women's suffrage if in power. Upon receiving no answer, they ask again – this time louder. The pair are thrown out and, in the struggle, they spit on the policeman. Both are imprisoned: Christabel is subjected to seven days' imprisonment, and Annie to 3 days in the notorious Strangeways' Gaol. This stint in prison does not deter the two from causing disruption at further Liberal party meetings.

The image here shows both Annie Kenney and Christabel Pankhurst after their first spell in prison in 1906, and just before the WSPU moves its headquarters from Manchester to London to target more ministers.

Annie Kenney and Christabel Pankhurst are leading figures in the WSPU. This image is taken shortly after their first arrest for disrupting a Liberal Party meeting in 1905.
COPY 1/494

Adela Pankhurst disrupts many political meetings near Manchester. She regularly addresses large crowds at public meetings for women's votes.
COPY 1/528

Manchester, though, remains a hub for heckling, with Adela Pankhurst taking a prominent role. Churchill is a popular target, and endures a spate of interruptions from Adela and various other suffragists during several of his speeches. On one occasion, seven women scatter themselves amongst the audience, with hats covering their faces, and take it in turns to disrupt him. One by one they rise, unfurl a 'Votes for Women' banner – like the one Annie Kenney and Christabel Pankhurst are holding in the image – and demand to know his position on women's rights to vote. One after another, they are thrown out and arrested.

Christabel and Annie deliberately use their arrests as opportunities to bolster publicity for the WSPU. In their deliberate pursuit of imprisonment, they successfully manage to deflect focus from the content of the speeches and on to the plight of women. The 'Votes for Women' banners become instantly recognisable, and a simple, yet effective, slogan for the party.

As reactions to the women get heavy handed and sentencing increasingly severe, there is some public sympathy for the women. The NUWSS show open support to the WSPU's efforts to raise awareness of female suffrage. The Press, though, is less sympathetic, and the Daily Mail disparagingly coins the name 'Suffragettes', intended figuratively to belittle them. The women, though, quite pleased with their own nickname, reclaim the name for themselves.

Through these tactics, Votes for Women is firmly in the spotlight for the first time. WSPU membership is on the rise.

Some members of the WSPU are growing agitated at the perceived autocracy of the Pankhursts and their leadership team. In protest, they form the Women's Freedom League (WFL) in 1907, a democratic group that prefers the less controversial methods of passive resistance.

The Suffragettes continue to incite interruptions at political meetings, but the Liberals soon get wise to this. Addresses become ticketed events only and ministers are driven there, leaving fewer opportunities for Suffragettes to jeer ministers. The women must adapt tactics. They begin to plan larger and bolder protests.

With a change to the Liberal leadership, the Suffragettes must now contend with an added obstacle in the form of the new Prime Minister, Herbert Henry Asquith – a staunch opponent of women's rights. Emmeline plans a "rush" on the House of Commons and a handbill is issued inciting crowds to join. She does make a last-ditch attempt to move forward through a more peaceful and diplomatic approach, and writes a letter to Asquith, urging him to bring female suffrage to the new parliament. When Asquith responds that this will not be discussed, Emmeline springs into action. On 11 October 1908, Emmeline and Christabel Pankhurst, together with Flora Drummond, each address an excited crowd in Trafalgar Square, urging them to 'come unarmed, and without sticks or stones' but to lend their support to women's votes and join an organised rush on the House of Commons two days later.

The police are forewarned and, fearing that a "rush" is synonymous with violence and public unrest, summon the three to court the next day for 'inciting the public to do a certain and wrongful and illegal act, to rush the House of Commons.' The three women refuse, and, in a further act of defiance, Christabel sends a response to the summons, outlining that they would only be available the day after, the 13th, at 6pm for arrest.

After reportedly spending the day relaxing in Flora Drummond's garden, the women head to the WSPU Headquarters at the hour specified by Christabel, where Inspector Jarvis and his officers are waiting for them. He reads the women a warrant and promptly arrests them. Whilst in custody, 60,000 people – men and women, suffragettes, opponents and intrigued spectators – gather in Parliament Square at the advertised 7:30pm. The police are expecting them. Dozens of women are arrested, and only one woman manages to make it past the huge police presence to reach the House of Commons. She storms into a chamber where a group of MPs are deliberating other matters and demands that they instead discuss votes for women – much to their bemusement. She is quickly arrested.

This action, and the subsequent trials of both the leaders and direct participants, arouses a high level of press attention. Although the 'rush' does pose a genuine cause of concern,

The 1908 'rush' on Parliament by Suffragettes produces a range of responses in the media. Postcards like this one are produced mocking the Suffragettes for their 'unladylike' actions. *COPY 1/526*

many, encouraged by the Press and government, still do not take the Suffragettes as seriously as their actions suggest. In fact, the 'rush' and the subsequent trial present publishers and cartoonists with the perfect opportunity for ridiculing the notion of female suffrage. Anti-suffrage photographs, publications and postcards are in abundance.

The 'Suffragette series' of 1908 soon becomes one of the most recognised. The series features an actor dressed as a Suffragette, recreating the latest spectacle of the 'rush' on parliament. The depiction is not flattering. Quite literally in this portrayal they are men; the actors are playing on, no doubt to appeal to public opinion, the familiar argument that Suffragettes are not 'real' women; they are sexual and moral deviants, old and ugly spinsters who simply cannot find a husband. They are the antithesis of the ideal Edwardian female. Their 'mad' actions of the 'rush', clearly ridiculed in the postcards, are proof of female hysteria, and the women have clearly shown through irrational logic and justification of their methods that they could never be trusted with the vote. The cure for hysteria and lesbianism is not the vote, but to find them a man! If they had a man, after all, women surely wouldn't be transgressing prescribed, 'natural' gender roles and demanding the same rights as men!

Partly in response to these mixed reactions, the pamphlet 'The Trial of the Suffragette Leaders', produced by Frederick Pethwick-Lawrence in 1909, is written to gain support for the WSPU, to discredit the Liberal government by giving 'a full account of the case in an accessible form'; and to reclaim a sense of credibility for the movement.

The pamphlet celebrates the 'brilliant conduct of the case by Christabel' as a triumph for the WSPU. Drawing on her training as a lawyer, she contests the use of the term 'rush' – directly challenging two government ministers who believe it was deliberately chosen to incite violence. Christabel is well prepared: armed with a dictionary, she retorts that it is defined only as an 'earnest demand', a 'hurry', or an 'earnest pressure of business' with no reference to violence at all. Do they not, Christabel asks, have a habit of 'rushing' bills through parliament? Despite her best efforts, the women are found guilty and sentenced. Emmeline and Flora are imprisoned for three months, and Christabel escapes with a slightly lesser sentence of ten weeks in Holloway. The trial, the pamphlet declares, has exposed the government's 'direct attack…upon the leaders of the women's movement' and their attempt to 'break down by coercive measures the agitation for constitutional rights'. The rush is presented as a justified and constitutional means to gain support for suffrage; the government are illegally quashing these rights by arresting the women involved.

The severity of the sentences attracts yet more public criticism of the government, bolstering the claims made in the pamphlet that the government is the enemy of the constitution. The press and WSPU pamphlets help to rouse more women to the fight, and risk arrest, for the cause.

THE TRIAL
OF THE
SUFFRAGETTE
LEADERS

Kindly lent by the London News Agency.]

Inspector Jarvis reading the Warrant.

PUBLISHED BY
THE WOMAN'S PRESS, 4, CLEMENTS INN, STRAND, W.C.

PRICE ONE PENNY.

The trial of Christabel and Emmeline Pankhurst, and Flora Drummond, arrested for inciting the 'rush' on Parliament, provokes a high level of media interest. This pamphlet aims to both capitalise on the interest in the Suffragettes, but also aims to discredit the Liberal government for their 'direct attack' on the Suffragette leaders. *PRO 30/69/1834*

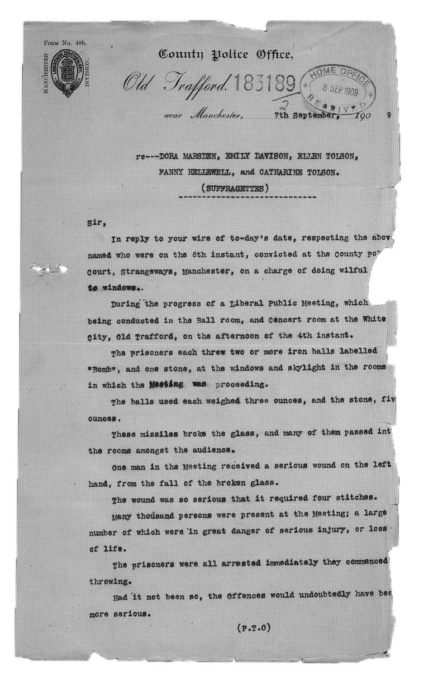

Form No. 48b.

County Police Office,

Old Trafford. 183189

near Manchester, 7th September, 190 9

HOME OFFICE
8 SEP 1909
RECEIVED

re---DORA MARSDEN, EMILY DAVISON, ELLEN TOLSON,
FANNY HELLEWELL, and CATHARINE TOLSON.
(SUFFRAGETTES)

Sir,

In reply to your wire of to-day's date, respecting the abov
named who were on the 6th instant, convicted at the County Po
Court, Strangeways, Manchester, on a charge of doing wilful
to windows..

During the progress of a Liberal Public Meeting, which
being conducted in the Ball room, and Concert room at the White
City, Old Trafford, on the afternoon of the 4th instant.

The prisoners each threw two or more iron balls labelled
"Bomb", and one stone, at the windows and skylight in the rooms
in which the Meeting was proceeding.

The balls used each weighed three ounces, and the stone, fiv
ounces.

These missiles broke the glass, and many of them passed int
the rooms amongst the audience.

One man in the Meeting received a serious wound on the left
hand, from the fall of the broken glass.

The wound was so serious that it required four stitches.

Many thousand persons were present at the Meeting; a large
number of which were in great danger of serious injury, or loss
of life.

The prisoners were all arrested immediately they commenced
throwing.

Had it not been so, the Offences would undoubtedly have bee
more serious.

(P.T.O)

This report from Lancashire police is sent to the Home Office on 7th September 1909. It describes the actions of five Suffragettes, including Emily Davison, who smash windows of a building during a Liberal party meeting in Manchester. They are arrested and sentenced to prison.

HO 144/1041/183189 Reproduced with kind permission from Lancashire Constabulary.

WSPU members are outraged by the government's attack on women and the denial of their constitutional rights by protest. Without any official instruction, women nationwide intensify the violence. Dora Marsden, Emily Davison, Ellen and Catharine Tolson, and Fanny Hellewell, are amongst hundreds of women across the country, who embark on a destructive campaign of spontaneous window smashing. Lead balls labelled 'bomb', and stones are hurled through the windows of an Old Trafford venue in Manchester, in a deliberate and targeted attack on the Liberal government, who are hosting a meeting there before 'many thousands' of supporters. One man receives injuries to his hand 'so serious it required four stitches.' The police are quick to the scene and arrest the women, to prevent more 'serious injury, or loss of life.' The five women are sentenced to serve time in Strangeways prison.

It is only when the WSPU employ more extreme and daring tactics, such as stone-throwing and deliberate acts of vandalism targeted at government property, that the government finally sits up and takes notice of women's suffrage and the lengths women are prepared to go. The government is forced into action.

As certain Suffragettes become repeat offenders, and individuals are prepared to break the law in open displays of their outrage, more police officers are assigned to keep tabs on them. In 1909, the Special Branch of the Criminal Investigation Department, originally established in 1884 to deal with suspected Irish and foreign terrorists in Britain, is expanded, to track Suffragette movements – such is the government's fear of suffragette disturbances and, what they believe to be, criminal activities. The Special Branch soon finds its hands full and requests an increase of 14 officers. This request is approved and soon there are over 20 officers assigned 'for the protection of the Ministers, but also for […] the public attending the meetings whose safety is wantonly endangered by the proceedings of the suffragettes.' This is not an insignificant number, considering that WSPU membership is relatively small – never peaking beyond 5,000.

Arrests and fines are becoming commonplace. Never in British history have women been targeted so proactively; but never has an organised group of British women been prepared to rebel against the authorities in so fierce a manner.

Despite government emphasis on tracking and arresting women, they severely underestimate the unshakeable conviction of many of these women. Although the Pankhursts' can claim no credit for issuing instructions to smash windows, an increasing number of individual women are employing more forceful and attention-grabbing tactics on their own initiative. It seems many women are not in the least bit deterred at the prospect of arrest and will actively choose imprisonment over paying a fine or signing a declaration of acquittal to forego militancy.

Marion Wallace Dunlop is one such individual who does not need to await instructions from the Pankhursts. She embarks on her own premeditated quest to cause commotion

Whilst imprisoned in Holloway prison for 'wilful damage', Marion Wallace Dunlop sends this petition to Herbert Gladstone, the Home Secretary. She is outraged that she is being treated as a common criminal, rather than as a political prisoner. *HO 144/1038/180965* are illegal". I understand that my sentence is for "wilful damage".

I wish to deny most earnestly any intention whatsoever of wilful damage.

I claim that my action in thus placing on the walls of the "House of the People" a reminder of the right of the people, was fully justified by reason of the fact that Mr. Asquith (the King's proxy) has persistently (by his refusal to receive women's deputations) violated this right.

I claim that the words which I printed are in themselves a proof that my action was entirely a political one. I therefore demand that you use your authority either to have me released, or else to have me placed in the 1st division in Holloway instead of in the 2nd division.

I demand too that you should require some explanation from the Magistrate at Bow Street of his action in classing a prisoner charged with a political offence in the 3rd division.

Yours faithfully

Marion Wallace-Dunlop

to bolster attention for the suffrage cause. On 24 June 1909, Marion, accompanied by Victor Duvel, a keen supporter of women's suffrage, enters parliament for the second time in a week and demands to see an MP. Since women are no longer permitted in the lobby – for fear of Suffragette actions – Marion waits in the hallway whilst Victor accompanies the Sergeant at Arms to get an MP. Being alone, she seizes the moment to hurriedly rubber stamp a quote onto the wall. Referring to the 1689 Bill of Rights, the quote reads, 'It is the right of the Subjects to petition the King and all commitments and prosecutions for such actions are illegal.' In other words, quashing women's marches and deputations to parliament is illegal.

She cannot escape quickly enough and is caught on both occasions by the returning Sergeant at Arms. On the second occasion, she is arrested and sentenced to one month's imprisonment in Holloway. She is outraged and denies 'most earnestly any intention whatsoever of "wilful damage."'

It is in prison that she mounts a new way to protest the government's treatment of Suffragettes as Second Division prisoners, usually reserved for common criminals. She demands to be treated as a First Division, political prisoner. She petitions to Herbert Gladstone, as Home Secretary, to 'use his authority to have [her] released, or else have [her] placed in the First Division'. Her actions, she maintains, were politically driven, intended to act as 'a reminder of the rights as people', which Asquith, the King's representative as Prime Minister has persistently violated.

As a common criminal, Marion – and the hundreds of other suffragettes arrested, are deprived of certain rights and privileges reserved for political prisoners. Their visiting rights are limited to one a fortnight, they are denied reading and writing materials to send letters home, and are subjected to more brutal treatment from prison guards. Sanitary conditions are reported to be so terrible that the Home Office is forced to investigate on numerous occasions from 1908 onwards. Keen to prove his prison guards are not ill-treating prisoners, the Governor of Holloway reports indignantly 'the statement that the hygiene conditions of the prison is quite contrary to fact' and it is 'quite untrue that coats with vermin in them were ever supplied.' He firmly denies any mistreatment on the behalf of his staff towards suffragette prisoners despite the 'conduct of these prisoners [trying] the temper of these wardresses very severely.'

Despite investigations regarding the prison conditions, the continued treatment of Suffragettes as criminal, rather than political, prisoners proves to be controversial for both the WSPU. The public, too, show an unusual level of sympathy at their plight. Until Gladstone moves Marion Wallace Dunlop into the First Division, she resolves 'as a matter of principle…to refuse all food until the matter is settled to [her] satisfaction' – to the incredulity of the Home Office. She is true to her word.

H. M. Prison, Holloway September 24 1908.

MEMORANDUM.

1. The statement that the hygienic condition of the prison is appalling is quite contrary to fact, and quite inconsistent with the health standard maintained amongst prisoners.

2. The water jugs, which are filled by prisoners themselves at the taps, contain 5 pints (good). They have been filled for Suffragettes regularly three times a day, and at any other time at the request of the prisoners. There is no stinting of water for any prisoner.

3. Prisoners are never given dirty clothes to wear. It is quite untrue that combs with vermin in them were ever supplied to them. All combs and brushes issued to them were clean, and generally new.

No. 345
(7345)

Holloway prison is forced to respond to concerns of the treatment of imprisoned Suffragettes. They challenge complaints that the prison conditions are unhygienic and that Suffragettes are being mistreated. *HO 144/882/1627074*

H. M. Prison,	190 .

MEMORANDUM.

As an illustration of this complaint I may point out that on one occasion a Suffragette complained to the Chairman of the Visiting Committee that her hair brush had vermin in it. The brush in question had been actually issued new from Store, and a careful examination of it satisfied the Chairman that the "vermin" was merely a speck of white in the make of the bristle.

A few cases, I may add, have been found amongst former batches of Suffragettes who had verminous heads on reception.

4. It is not correct that only one visit out of the cell is allowed in 24 hours at a fixed time. This has never been the case. I quote from the letter of

No. 345
(7345)

MEMORANDUM.

3

a former prisoner, Sarah Benett, addressed
to the Nation in February. 1908 the following
on this subject:- " I felt for them (the wardresses)
very much in the miles they had to walk
answering bells in the evening."

5. Neither is it correct that cell chambers
are emptied only once in 24 hours.

6. None of the batches of Suffragettes have
had socks or stockings to darn recently.
The first or second batch a year or two ago
may have had some given to them for repair,
but socks and stockings are invariably
washed before they are sent out for this purpose.
I cannot recall any complaint being made
of such a grievance at the time, and it is
obviously very difficult to meet such complaints after so long an interval - a remark
which applies equally to many of the

allegations that are made by their advocates outside rather than by the prisoners themselves.

I should like to add that I have always endeavoured to show these prisoners consideration and forbearance, that I do not know any instance of brutality or anything like it shown by wardresses, and that although the conduct of these prisoners has often been of a kind to try the temper of officers very severely.

P. G. Brunton
Governor

P.S. Shortly after my arrival in Holloway I was told that I was to be removed from the 3rd division to the 2nd I claim the right recognized by all civilized nations that a person imprisoned for a political offence should have 1st division treatment; & as a matter of principle not only for my own sake but for the sake of others who may come after me, I am now refusing all food untill this matter is settled to my satisfaction

Signed Marion Wallace-Dunlop

Marion Wallace Dunlop is the first Suffragette to go on hunger strike in protest of her treatment as a common criminal. She refuses food for 91 hours before she is released on health grounds. Hundreds of Suffragettes follow her example. *HO 144/1038/180905*

Doctors and prison warders warn the Home Office that she has refused all food for 91 hours, discretely throwing some out of the window. Her zeal, in disregard to pleas to stop her 'foolish behaviour', is to such an extent that she is labelled a fanatic by the authorities for her adamant belief that if she died in prison 'it would be a great thing for the cause.' The authorities fear she could become a martyr, and a backlash could ensue if they allow her to die in prison. They release her on health grounds. She is greeted with a heroes' welcome home from fellow Suffragettes.

The increase in militancy of the WSPU and WFL is becoming a pressing concern for some of their fellow comrades, as early as 1909. When Mrs Moore, a member of the WFL herself, receives a letter informing her of the latest plans for militant actions by two of her friends, she is appalled; they are planning to shoot the Prime Minister at the next picket line. Whilst she will not betray her friends' names out of loyalty, she informs the police at once. The women, she advises the police, have recently taken to refining their shooting skills at a shooting range on Tottenham Court Road. She has tried to use her influence to manage their radical behaviour, directly interceding on occasion to 'remove them from the carriage entrance at the House of Commons, but she has found that their 'actions are getting out of hand.' The police take this letter extremely seriously; Mrs Moore is, after all, 'a married woman' - unlike the 'half-insane women' of the picket line preparing to commit 'something nearly amounting to conspiracy to murder.' The police are terrified for the safety of Asquith, but are unsure over the safest course of action. If they remove the picket line, they would have to make the reason public. Furthermore, the removal might be 'be looked on by them as an act of violence and injustice' and tip the women over the edge to commit such a crime. If they don't remove the picket line, the Prime Minister's life is in jeopardy. Instead, seeing no other option, they redouble security efforts surrounding the picket and Asquith lives to see another day.

Women continue to be arrested. Believing they have found a way to humiliate the government, numerous Suffragettes follow Marion Wallace-Dunlop's lead and go on hunger-strike. Laura Ainsworth, Patricia Woodlock, and Ellen Barwell are amongst nine women who embark on a hunger strike in Winson Green prison in Birmingham for their part in protesting against Asquith in September 1909.

It becomes a wide-spread phenomenon, and even Emmeline, Christabel and Sylvia Pankhurst adopt this method whilst imprisoned. Medals are even issued to hunger-striking women in recognition of the suffering for the cause, spurring on yet more women to undertake hunger-striking. It presents a monumental problem for the government. Do they allow the women to starve and possibly die in prison? Should they attempt force feeding-usually reserved for those physically and mentally incapable of feeding themselves? Or do they just let the women go?

Releasing the Suffragettes early is both too humiliating and unviable a prospect, so they decide on forcible feeding. This is a huge miscalculation. Suffragettes who are released having undergone force feeding are quick to report their ordeal. To these women, fighting

To the Rt. Hon. H. H. Asquith,

Sir,

  We the undersigned, being medical practitioners, do most urgently protest against the treatment by artificial feeding of the Suffragist prisoners now in Birmingham Gaol.

  We submit to you, that this method of feeding when the patient resists is attended with the gravest risks, that unforeseen accidents are liable to occur, and that the subsequent health of the person may be seriously injured. In our opinion this action is unwise and inhumane.

  We therefore earnestly beg that you will interfere to prevent the continuance of this practice.

      We are, Sir,

       Yours faithfully,

      W Hugh W F Fenton
       M.D. M.A.

It is an absolutely beastly & revolting procedure. When patients resist the forced feeding it becomes positively dangerous. Sooner or later there will be fatal results & then there will be the usual whining excuses at the inquests of "brittle ribs" & "Status lymphaticus" as the predisposing cause of death. This method of coercion is after all more objectionable than anything the Suffragists have done on their own [W.H.F]

The practice of forced feeding appalls supporters and opponents of women's suffrage. This letter is sent by medical practitioners to the Prime Minister. They describe it as an 'absolutely beastly and revolting practice' and beg the Prime Minister to stop the continued practice.

HO 45/10417/183577

to be recognised as a person, with full control over their own bodies and minds, it represents an abhorrent violation; to some, it is considered akin to a form of rape.

Just as public sympathy for the women's movement seems to be dwindling in the face of their violent targeting of the government, force feeding turns out to be a propaganda gift for the WSPU. Pamphlets and publications declare it an 'act of torture'. The pamphlet overleaf, one of many produced by the WSPU, declares that, through this 'brutal feeding by force', the government has 'cast aside both law and humanity in dealing with women political prisoners'. This particular poster draws on the experiences of Leslie Hall and Selina Martin – although there are dozens of other pamphlets about force feeding of other women. Leslie and Selina are on remand in Walton Gaol, Liverpool, but when they refuse to take food in protest of their treatment as common criminals, officials threaten to subject them to force feeding. Upon hearing this, Selina Martin barricades herself in her cell, but officials 'fell upon her and handcuffed her, dragged her to a punishment cell and flung her on the floor, with her hands tightly fastened together behind her back' and force fed her. This caused 'intense suffering.' As the two women were technically on remand and therefore unconvicted prisoners, the government has broken the law. (See next page)

With another election brewing in 1910, the poster specifically targets male liberal supporters – as the only ones who have a political voice – to try to oust the Liberals from power. The Suffragettes are quick to exploit that many Liberal supporters are outraged by this violent intrusion on women as contrary to their liberal principles of fairness and democracy, or, as the WSPU put it, 'the political freedom which liberals profess to hold so dear'. In describing the Liberal government as 'the torturers of women', existing notions of gender also work in the women's favour for once, appealing to voters' notions of (liberal) masculinity and chivalry; women – even Suffragettes - are, after all, still 'the fairer sex'. The WSPU is hoping to sway votes and secure a Labour victory.

Amid election-fever, Lady Constance Lytton, a relatively late recruit to the WSPU, joining in 1909, is deeply disturbed by such revelations of force-feeding, which seem to be particularly brutal on working-class women. As an active reformer of prison conditions, she decides to test the theory. In January 1910, disguised as a working-class seamstress, Jane Wharton, she throws stones at a passing MP, in a deliberate act to get arrested. Her theory proves to be correct. Although prison is not a new experience for Lady Lytton, force feeding is. Imprisoned as an aristocrat, prison authorities never dared to subject her to it, but they seem to have no qualms when she is imprisoned under her working-class alias. She soon experiences its full brutality.

Upon discovery of her true identity, she is promptly released, which only serves to anger Lady Lytton further. Her stunt leaks out and Lady Lytton's working-class experience is soon picked up by the press. To expose the social injustices, she reveals how a tube was inserted down her throat and was relentlessly continued despite her existing heart condition and that

No. 64.

VOTES FOR WOMEN

The Women's Social and Political Union.

Head Office: 4, CLEMENTS INN, STRAND, W.C.

Telegraphic Address: "Wospo'u, London."

Telephone No. 2724 Holborn (three lines).

Founder and Hon. Secretary—Mrs. PANKHURST.
Joint Hon. Secretary—Mrs. TUKE.
Publishing Office—THE WOMAN'S PRESS.
Bankers—Messrs. BARCLAY & CO., Fleet Street, E.C.

Hon. Treasurer—Mrs. PETHICK LAWRENCE.
Organising Secretary—Miss CHRISTABEL PANKHURST, LL.B.
Newspaper—VOTES FOR WOMEN.
Colours—PURPLE, WHITE, & GREEN.

Atrocities in an English Prison.

Two Englishwomen, unconvicted prisoners on remand in an English prison (Walton Gaol, Liverpool), have been assaulted, knocked down, gagged, fed by force, kept for consecutive days and nights in irons.   One of them has been **frog-marched**. Frog-marched! What does that mean? Read the story.

The Facts.

On December 20th Miss Selina Martin and Miss Leslie Hall were arrested in Liverpool, and were remanded for one week, **bail being refused.**

Accordingly, while **still unconvicted prisoners**, they were sent to Walton Gaol, Liverpool. There, contrary to regulations, intercourse with their friends was denied to them. As unconvicted prisoners they refused to submit to the prison discipline or to take the prison food. Forcible feeding was threatened and Miss Martin therefore barricaded her cell. The officials, however, effected an entrance, fell upon her and handcuffed her, dragged her to a punishment cell and flung her on the floor, with her hands tightly fastened together behind her back.

Frog-Marched.

All that night she was **kept in irons.** Next day her cell was entered, she was seized, thrown down over with her face upon the floor. In this position, face downwards, her arms and legs were dragged up her till she was lifted from the ground. Her hair was seized by another wardress. In this way "frog-marched" up the steps to the doctor's room, **her head bumping on the stone stairs.** In the room the operation of forcible feeding was performed—causing intense suffering—and then this tortured a terrible state of physical and mental distress, was handcuffed again, flung down the steps and pushed dragged back into her cell. Her companion, Leslie Hall, was kept in irons for two and a half consecutive and nights.

What was the Charge against Miss Martin?

What terrible crime had Miss Martin done? She had dared to protest against the political slavery of her sex; against the refusal of the Prime Minister to receive any Deputation from women; and against the exclusion of women from political meetings. The charge against Miss Martin was that she had thrown an empty ginger-beer bottle at an empty motor-car—the car that had taken Mr. Asquith to the meeting. But when she was treated in this terribly cruel way these charges had not been proved, she was "on remand," and by the theory of English law presumed innocent. Bail had been offered, she was ready to give an undertaking that no disturbance should take place during the week for which the case was remanded. **Bail was arbitrarily refused** in spite of the fact that though there have been hundreds of Suffragette prisoners, they have never attempted to escheat their bail.

The frog march, and the other assaults and cruelties, the brutal feeding by force, were resorted to during this week of remand, **while she was an unconvicted prisoner.** Prison officials, encouraged by the Government, have cast aside both law and humanity in dealing with women political prisoners.

Is this England?

If such deeds were done in Russia there would be an outcry in this country. Are they to be tolerated here?

Electors! You and you only can put a stop to this terrible injustice. These two women are in prison **now.** Miss Martin is sentenced to two months' hard labour and Miss Hall to one month.

Electors! assert your will. Secure the release of these women who have already suffered such horr torture. It can be done by voting against the Government which is responsible for this cruelty. The pri authorities are the tools of the Government, and act as they are bidden by the Home Office. Because wo are making their cry heard for that political freedom which Liberals profess to hold so dear in the case of m the Liberal Government is persecuting them with unheard of violence and cruelty.

Electors, vote against the Liberal Candidate in your Constituency, for if returned he will go into Parliament to support Mr. Asquith and his Government, who are the torturers of women.

Vote against the Government and keep the Liberal out!

Read our paper, "VOTES FOR WOMEN," One Penny Weekly.

Copies of this leaflet can be obtained from The Woman's Press, price 9d. a hundred, 6/- a thousand, post free.

Published by THE WOMEN'S SOCIAL AND POLITICAL UNION, 4, Clements Inn, Strand, W.C., and Printed by ST. CLEMENTS PRESS, LTD., Portugal Street, W C.

HO 144/1052

The WSPU are quick to publish information on the ordeals of those who have experienced forced feeding. This leaflet describes the ordeal of Selina Martin and Leslie Hall, who are forced fed whilst in Walton Gaol, Liverpool in 1909. The leaflets aims to encourage men to vote against the Liberal party in the 1910 election. *HO 144/1052/187234* she was violently throwing up. She endured this, she reports, eight times during her two-week sentence. She writes a letter to Herbert Gladstone, putting forward her abhorrence of her discoveries and urging an immediate stop to the practice of force feeding.

Accounts such as Lytton's, on the brutality of the act permeates public consciousness. Forced feeding is already an unpopular method amongst the public and the WSPU seek to play on this embedded unpopularity to increase public sympathy for the cause and public opposition to the government.

In the days before the election, some Suffragettes take to protesting outside polling stations. Accounts of force feeding perhaps do leave an impression on some of the male electorate; the Liberal government, although re-elected, loses numerous seats and their majority is considerably weakened.

Soon after their re-election, a Conciliation Bill is drafted and sent to parliament for approval. The Bill aims to extend the vote to some property-holding women. It is approved for a second reading and it looks, for a short while, that the Suffrage movement can declare a partial victory. The WSPU call a truce to their militant actions whilst they await the verdict. Asquith, however, soon dashes all hopes of triumph for the women and makes it clear that the Bill will not become law. The WSPU is furious. The truce ends abruptly and the Pankhursts announce that militancy is now more a necessity than ever.

In response to the betrayal, Princess Sophia Duleep-Singh (an exiled Indian Princess) and Emmeline Pankhurst lead a congregation of over 300 women to the House of Commons. The government, though, are prepared; police line the streets and have orders to stop the women reaching parliament. Two women throw stones at Asquith's house and vandalise his car in expressions of their anger, and some women are reported to kick policemen and passing government ministers. The police, and numerous male onlookers, interpret orders to stop the women as a stamp of approval to use undue force. Violent scenes erupt; approximately 200 women are physically assaulted, and dozens more are deliberately groped and sexually assaulted. Suffragette accounts documenting the violence are reprinted in some left-wing newspapers alongside photos, such as this one. The left-wing press seize the opportunity to undermine the Liberal government who, the papers claim, ordered excessive force against defenceless women. In this image, opposite, Ernestine Mills, lying on the floor, has her hands covering her face, which, some newspapers report, is due to the fear of violence from the policeman leaning over her in an intimidating fashion. The Houses of Parliament, a symbol of British democracy, can be seen just feet away in the background, standing in sharp contrast to the violence happening around it. The government demands that such photos are withdrawn, but the damage has been done. Some of the public are disgusted at the levels of violence resorted to by the police on orders from the government. Others, however, dismiss the violence as a necessary response to the Suffragettes' hysteria. The event goes down in Suffragette history as 'Black Friday.' 130 women file complaints against the police for acts of brutality. The 115 women and four men who have

This photograph is believed to be of Ernestine Mills during demonstrations outside the Houses of Parliament in November 1910. Because the police are accused of brutality and violence towards Suffragettes, the event becomes known as 'Black Friday'. *COPY 1/551*

been arrested, are released without charge on the advice of Churchill – who is keen to avoid a public inquiry into the police actions. At least two women die of the injuries they sustain days later. Emmeline's sister, Mary, also dies - reportedly also due to police mistreatment and her subsequent stint in prison. Reputational damage is done to both sides. Not wanting to expose themselves to this level of violence again, WSPU tactics change once more.

Although the WSPU (and some WFL) militancy attracts the bulk of the headlines, other Suffrage societies are working more quietly in the background. The NUWSS and the WFL, initially supportive of the WSPU's more unconventional and confrontational stance on the matter, distance themselves from the militant tactics as they get increasingly violent. Instead, they, like other Suffrage organisations, seek a more peaceful resolution to the dispute over female suffrage.

The Suffragists Vigilance League, a small peripheral suffrage society, (politely) warn the government 'of the very grave risk that is now being run by them in their treatment of

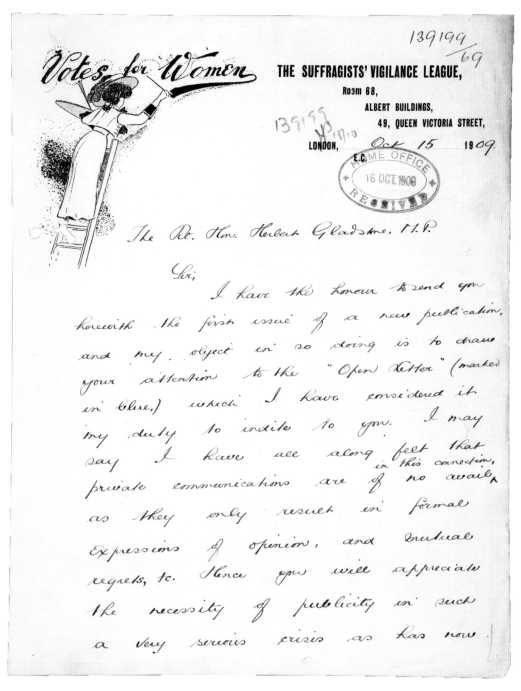

Votes for Women

THE SUFFRAGISTS' VIGILANCE LEAGUE,

Room 68,

ALBERT BUILDINGS,

49, QUEEN VICTORIA STREET,

LONDON,   Oct 15   1909.

139199/69

13919̄5 /1910

HOME OFFICE
16 OCT 1909
RECEIVED

The Rt. Hon. Herbert Gladstone, M.P.

Sir,

I have the honour to send you herewith the first issue of a new publication, and my object in so doing is to draw your attention to the "Open Letter" (marked in blue,) which I have considered it my duty to indite to you. I may say I have all along felt that in this connection, private communications are of no avail, as they only result in formal expressions of opinion, and mutual regrets, &c. Hence you will appreciate the necessity of publicity in such a very serious crisis as has now

There are many suffrage organisations nationwide. The Suffragists' Vigilance League publish their own paper, The Suffragist, in 1909 and send a copy to the Home Secretary, Herbert Gladstone.
HO 45/10338/139199

women suffragists.' In the name of peace and justice, they urge a '"round table conference" [to] discuss matters in a quiet and amicable spirit.' They also take the liberty of sending the Home Office a copy of the first publication of their newspaper, The Suffragist. Perhaps they hope to show the irrational nature of anti-suffrage opposition through their feature, 'Why I Am Opposed to Female Suffrage', which satirises the anti-suffrage arguments, including those made by many government ministers. Herbert Henry Asquith is a natural target of ridicule and his reasoning behind opposing female enfranchisement is mentioned on several occasions. In a particularly witty response to the mocking claim made by anti-suffragists that 'no woman has given to the world any worth of permanent value', the Editor remarks 'is Asquith of no value, eh?'

The WFL also approaches the government with a more familiar method. It continues to petition the Prime Minister and ask him on numerous occasions to accept a deputation to receive its petitions. Asquith refuses on all counts.

In frustration, it, like the WSPU, resorts to historical precedents to make its point, and asserts its constitutional rights to petition the King as outlined in the 1689 Bill of Rights. In July 1909, it calls for direct intervention from Edward VIII to settle 'the constitutional difference' on this right. Its demands are numerous but nothing new. It seeks to point out the unfairness of parliamentary exclusion as women have 'directly and indirectly [contributed] to the national taxation; they do their duties of 'unwearying labour in the home'; and contribute 'valuable yet underpaid' employment and public service to the poor, education and the sick. Referencing the severity of the sentences of Suffragettes arrested on, what they consider, lawful protests and demonstrations, they are concerned that suffragists have suffered 'unlawful imprisonment' and 'degradation meted out to common criminals.' The biggest sticking point – unsurprisingly – is that 'being voteless [they] have no other way of making known [their] grievance' – especially as constitutional methods of petition are being repudiated by the government.

To their dismay, the king declines to see them. Out of sheer frustration, Charlotte Despard, leader of the WFL, and eight other members, drive to the Home Office bearing the WFL's banners to present the petition and demand, in line with the Bill of Rights, that they see the King to 'secure their right to petition.' The king's private secretary, Lord Knollys, reluctantly agrees to see them, but conversations, once again, amount to nothing.

In support of the WFL's quest to petition directly to the king, the Men's Committee for Justice to Women, founded in January 1909, also requests to present their petition to the king. Whilst in support of enfranchisement for women, the men's objectives are driven more out of a desire for justice, which they fear is being denied to women who are being 'wrongfully imprisoned', severely sentenced 'contrary to the weight of evidence' and treated as common criminals. Referring to the WFL's refusal to lay their grievances before the

139 199/64

VOTES FOR WOMEN.

WOMEN'S FREEDOM LEAGUE.

OBJECTS.—To secure for Women the Parliamentary Vote as it is or may be granted to men; to use the power thus obtained to establish equality of rights and opportunities between the sexes, and to promote the social and industrial well-being of the community.

President:
MRS. C. DESPARD.
Hon. Treasurer:
MISS S. BENETT.

Hon. Organising Secretary:
MRS. T. BILLINGTON-GREIG.
Hon. Secretary:
MRS. HOW MARTYN, A.R.C.S., B.Sc.

Auditor:
E. AYRES PURDIE, A.L.A.A.,
Certified Accountant,
52, Craven House, Kingsway.

Office Hours—10 till 5.
Saturdays—10 till 1.

TELEPHONE: 15143 CENTRAL.
TELEGRAMS: "TACTICS," LONDON.

OFFICE: **1, Robert Street,
Adelphi, Strand, W.C.**

15th July,   190 9.

Right Hon. Herbert Gladstone, M.P.,

Sir,

Your letter of the 12th July has been considered by myself and my colleagues of the Women's Freedom League. We beg to call your attention to the fact that your refusal to advise His Majesty to receive us is based upon a misconception of our purpose. We desire an audience of His Majesty the King in order to urge upon him the wrong that is at present done to us by the refusal of His Majesty's Prime Minister to receive us. Our statutory right entitles us to a hearing from the King, constitutional custom has transferred the duty of receiving petitioners to the Prime Minister, the most responsible member of the House of Commons. If we are denied a hearing by the latter, to the former we must appeal.

We beg to remind you that this point was made clear when you received our deputation on Thursday, July 8th, and you yourself, after reading the petition we placed in your hands, stated that "it was an argued plea for an audience."

Men's Committee for Justice to Women.

139199/65ᵃ

Forwarded by the King Mags to
10 Downing St. and thence by
Mr Nash.

[HOME OFFICE RECEIVED 29.7.08]

133 Salisbury Sq.
London. E.C.
July 24. 09.

To His Most Excellent Majesty King Edward VII.

On the 29th of June last we sought to place a Petition before Your Majesty. and in accordance with the instructions so courteously given on that occasion by Lord Knollys we approached Your Majesty through the Home Office. But the Petition has through this channel failed to achieve its object, and we humble and loyal subjects of Your Majesty again beg to approach you with a simple plea for Justice.

Certain of Your Majesty's subjects being women whilst seeking in a constitutional manner to lay before Your Majesty's Prime Minister the need for the enfranchisement of their sex have been wrongfully arrested, convicted in Your Majesty's Police Courts under the summary jurisdiction of a single Stipendary Magistrate contrary to the weight of evidence harshly sentenced and treated as criminal offenders in Your Majesty's Prison at Holloway.

A large number of women subjects of Your Majesty have suffered injustice in this way and at the present time some are undergoing imprisonment in the Second Division.

We in all sincerity submit to

As petitions are largely being ignored by Asquith and the government, the Women's Freedom League ask for an audience with King Edward VII so that they can present their petitions directly to him. When this is refused, the Men's Committee for Justice to Women also make known their concerns regarding the 'injustice' being shown towards Suffragettes. HO 45/10338/139199

King, they take up the fight of female suffrage on behalf of the voiceless women. Echoing the WFL's demands, they deplore the King to 'ensure a reception of a Woman's Deputation' by the Prime Minister, treat imprisoned suffragists as First Division prisoners; and 'ensure justice' to those women 'unselfishly giving their liberty and lives to a cause sacred to them.' Interestingly, they do not ask that female suffrage is granted. These pleas, like so many others before, fall on deaf ears, and their plea is refused.

It cannot have been lost on the WFL – nor on any other suffrage society – that petitioning has, once again, failed to progress women's rights. The WFL is feeling increasingly let down by the government. Having tried and, again, failed to reason with the government via constitutional methods, the WFL plans a more disruptive protest: it will cause maximum commotion at the forthcoming 1910 elections. Instructions are issued to its members to plan for 'attendance at every polling station' where they will hold meetings outside and prevent 'antis' from entering. If taxation is the qualification for voting, women will also bring along tax papers and demand to be allowed to vote. Their plan is foiled by police who are forewarned. The WFL re-thinks its strategy once more.

1911 presents a prime opportunity. The WFL concoct a plan that will involve participation from more women than ever before, and cause more trouble for the government: they will boycott the census.

In a deviation from previous census returns, the 1911 census will ask, for the first time, how long people have been married and how many children women have borne – both alive and dead. The government is concerned about the effects of working women on birth and mortality rates. Suffragists and Suffragettes alike immediately go on the defensive and assume the worst, believing the government intends to take away the small gains women have made and limit women's employment to 'save' Britain from declining birth rates.

The WFL, in cooperation with the WSPU and NUWSS, appeals to women everywhere to oppose the government by shunning the census. Protests and marches are organised up and down the country. Rallying cries of 'No Vote, No Census', and 'If women don't count nor shall they be counted!' can be heard everywhere to rouse support for the boycott. Women respond in their thousands. The government, in desperation, promises a £5 fine to those women who refuse to participate in the census in a bid to put off as many working-class women as possible, but most remain undeterred. As census night looms nearer, tensions are running high.

On 2 April 1911, enumerators up and down the country are faced with a more arduous task than usual. They are confronted with taunts and obstructions from women as they knock on doors to collect census returns. They receive no answer at all from other houses as hundreds of women avoid being at home altogether and congregate at local parks. 'Census houses', such as those in Manchester, offer retreat to scores of census-evading women.

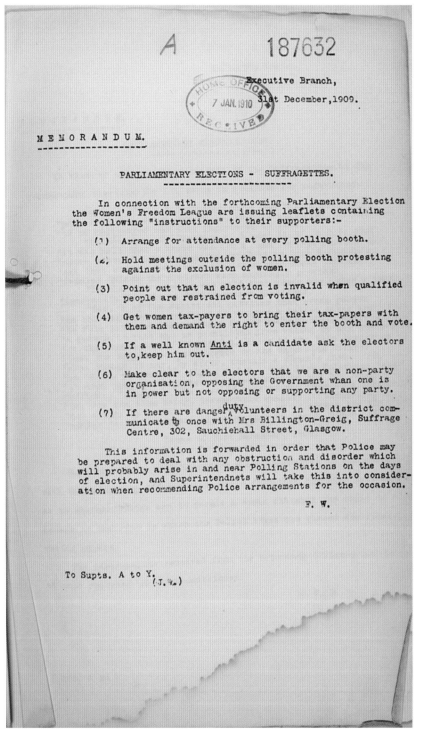

A 187632

Executive Branch,
31st December,1909.

HOME OFFICE
7 JAN. 1910
RECEIVED

M E M O R A N D U M.

PARLIAMENTARY ELECTIONS - SUFFRAGETTES.

In connection with the forthcoming Parliamentary Election the Women's Freedom League are issuing leaflets containing the following "instructions" to their supporters:-

(1) Arrange for attendance at every polling booth.

(2) Hold meetings outside the polling booth protesting against the exclusion of women.

(3) Point out that an election is invalid when qualified people are restrained from voting.

(4) Get women tax-payers to bring their tax-papers with them and demand the right to enter the booth and vote.

(5) If a well known Anti is a candidate ask the electors to,keep him out.

(6) Make clear to the electors that we are a non-party organisation, opposing the Government when one is in power but not opposing or supporting any party.

(7) If there are danger duty volunteers in the district communicate to once with Mrs Billington-Greig, Suffrage Centre, 302, Sauchiehall Street, Glasgow.

This information is forwarded in order that Police may be prepared to deal with any obstruction and disorder which will probably arise in and near Polling Stations on the days of election, and Superintendnets will take this into consideration when recommending Police arrangements for the occasion.

F. W.

To Supts. A to Y.
(J. W.)

In the 1910 elections, the Women's Freedom League issue leaflets urging women to cause disruption at polling booths in protest against the exclusion of women. The police are forewarned and the WFL fail to cause any major disruption to elections.

HO 45/10597/187632

apply Cannon Row Police Station for further information

CENSUS

OF

ENGLAND AND WALES,

1911.

SCHEDULE.

Prepared pursuant to the Census (Great Britain) Act, 1910.

This space to be filled up by the Enumerator.

Number of Registration District....... 5

Number of Registration Sub-District....... 3

Number of Enumeration District....... 24

Name of Head of Family or Separate Occupier. } .... *Miss E. W. Davidson*

Found hiding in

Postal Address....... *Crypt of*

Westminster Hall

WESTMINSTER

3/4/11

Since Saturday

NOTICE.

This Schedule must be filled up and signed by, or on behalf of, the Head of the Family or other person in occupation, or in charge, of the dwelling (house, tenement or apartment).

No. of Schedule.	Address.	Kind of Building. (For Blocks of Flats and Model Dwellings the Numbers of separate Flats or Tenements must be stated.)	Name of Occupier.	Dwellings or Tenements.			Buildings not used as dwellings.	Population.		
				In-habited.	Un-inhabited.	Build-ing.		Males.	Fe-males.	Per-sons.
1.	2.	3.	4.	5.	6.	7.	8.	9.	10.	11.
71	Cannon Row	Police Stn: Men's Quarters	Sergt. Dammarell	1				89	–	89
"	9	Shop					1			
	St. Margaret's Street	Church					1			
	Whitehall, Gwydd House	Offices					1			
	"	Royal United Service Institution					1			
	"	Museum					1			
72	1. Dean's Yard	Private House	Lady Newnes	1				1	5	6
73	2. Dean's Yard	Offices	G. Flegg	1				1	1	2
74	Houses of Parliament	Crypt	Miss E.W. Davidson	1					1	1
25	Victoria Embankment			1				10	–	10
	Scotland House, Horse Guards Avenue	Offices						1		
	5 Whitehall Court							1		
	End of Ecclesiastical Parish.									
	St. Margaret Westminster (part of) Civil Parish									
	St. Margaret & St. John (part of)									
		Total to be carried forward to Abstract		5				55	101	7	108

Emily Davison is found hiding in the crypt in Westminster Hall in the Houses of Commons and is recorded as the 'sole occupant'. Emily ends up being on the census twice as her landlady records her details. *RG 14/489*

Emily Wilding Davison takes to hiding in the chapel crypt of the House of Commons, seeking to avoid the enumerator altogether but knowing that, if caught, she can have the satisfaction that her address will have to be recorded as parliament. She is caught, and, as she had hoped, the enumerator records her address as 'Found Hiding in Crypt of Westminster Hall, Westminster, since Saturday' – the day before the census. The rest of the details, though, are recorded wrongly. In another ironic twist, her landlady at her address in London fills out Emily's correct details. Emily is therefore recorded twice, inadvertently skewing results for the government that is so desperately striving for accurate data.

Other women, unable to go into hiding, deface the census. Women in their hundreds scribble out their name, or scrawl messages across the page. Miss Davies, the head of a household, ironically informs the enumerator that there are 'no persons here, only women!' at her residence. Louisa Burnham, too, defaces the census, informing the government that 'if I am intelligent enough to fill out this census form, I can surely

The 1911 census boycott sees thousands of women nationwide deface their census papers. Here, the census information is covered with suffrage material encouraging the census boycott, and the message reads: 'no persons here, only women!' *RG 14/118* mark an X on a ballot paper'. Bertha Aryton similarly asks 'how can I answer all of these questions if I have not the intelligence to choose between two candidates?'. Bertha takes it a step further when she defies the enumerator directly, stating she will be prepared to give him the particulars required for the census only when certain promises are made by the government. Both Louisa and Bertha succeed in causing sufficient confusion to the officials, who ask the government if the enumerator should simply make up the schedule with the best details available. The government answer in the affirmative and, despite her efforts, Bertha's details, and those of her two servants, are recorded anyway.

Exasperated husbands, as the head of the household, are forced to apologise on behalf of their wives' efforts and overrule their objections on more than one occasion. Eleanora Maund's husband, Edward, puts his wife's attempt to 'defeat the purpose of the census' down to a 'silly sabotage'. He re-records Eleanora's details, which she has deliberately struck out, and states that 'it must stand as correct'. Eleanora's protest, therefore, whilst it does not go unnoticed, fails.

Eleanora Maund deliberately crosses out her name on the census entry recorded by her husband, Edward Arthur Maund. He re-enters her details and writes a note apologisng for his wife's actions of 'silly sabotage to defeat the object of the census.' Despite Eleanora's efforts, she is recorded on the census. RG 14/227

These women are amongst tens of thousands of women, largely upper and middle classes, but some of the working class, who respond to the WFL's pleas to boycott the census. There is a particularly high evasion rate in London. Due to the sheer scale of the boycott, no women, despite government promises, are arrested or fined, and the chaos is enough to attract huge amounts of publicity for the cause.

A month later, parliament passes another Conciliation Bill. Once again, it is abandoned. Yet another bill is laid before parliament in 1912, but this, too, is defeated. Battle lines between the two sides are hardened. The WSPU chooses to step up its militant campaign, in the hope that active resistance will achieve what passive resistance has so far failed to do: secure women the vote.

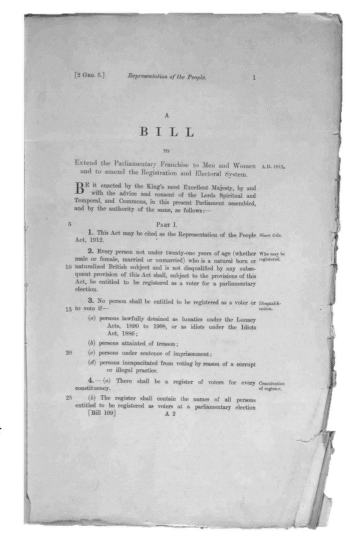

The inclusion of women to the 'Suffrage Bill' is laid before Parliament in 1912. It aims to give both men and women over the age of 21 the right to vote. The Prime Minister, Herbert Asquith, rejects the inclusion on the grounds that there is no proof it 'is really desired' and the Bill is rejected. The second reading is also defeated by **14 votes.** *HO 45/10612/194095/36*

CHAPTER 3

MORE DEEDS, LESS WORDS, 1913–1914

The year 1913 opens with a direct call for action from Emmeline Pankhurst to WSPU members. The government have promised, yet again, to discuss the addition of a women's suffrage amendment to the Franchise Bill for universal male suffrage. Having been repeatedly betrayed by the government so far, the WSPU is, understandably, sceptical, and Emmeline declares that it must be prepared for disappointment. In the instance of failure, militancy will become 'more a moral duty and more a political necessity than it has ever been before.' She urges women to let her know that they 'are ready to share in manifesting in a practical manner the indignation at the betrayal of our cause.' Women must 'be militant in some way or other.' If they are not, they will 'share responsibility for the crime' and be indirectly contributing to their own repression.

Hundreds rally behind the call to arms. When the Franchise Bill is dismissed in parliament, it effectively signals war. Militancy is stepped up. In war, Emmeline declares, the public must inevitably experience the seriousness of the situation and the lengths Suffragettes are willing to go to claim their constitutional rights and be recognised as citizens. Since March 1912, public buildings and shops in London's West End have been targeted a coordinated window smashing campaign.

However, it is no longer only government buildings and high-end shops targeted for window smashing. Public places and tourist attractions become prime targets; museums, cafes, and shops are attacked; communication lines are disrupted; and telephone wires and letterboxes destroyed. Arson becomes commonplace.

Suffragettes all over the country set to work. The Tower of London, Kew Gardens and St Paul's are amongst the first public places to suffer damage at the hands of Suffragette activists, who are hoping to force the government's hand due to the extremity of the situation.

Leonora Cohen, an active member of the Leeds branch of the WSPU, is in London to participate in a deputation to Lloyd-George. Here, she hears that Asquith has dropped the reform bill, and consequently she decides to stay on a few extra days, vowing to play her

EXHIBIT No.

VOTES FOR WOMEN.

The Women's Social and Political Union.

OFFICE: LINCOLN'S INN HOUSE, KINGSWAY, W.C.

Mrs. Pankhurst, Hon. Treasurer.
Mrs. Mabel Tuke, Hon. Sec.

All Communications,
unless marked "private" will be opened
by the Hon. Secretary.

Auditors: **Messrs. Sayers & Wesson,**
Chartered Accountants, 19. Hanover Square, W.

Telegraphic Address—WOSPOLU, LONDON.
Telephone 2724 Holborn (three lines).

January 10th, 1913.

Private and Confidential.

Dear Friend,

The Prime Minister has announced that in the week beginning January 20th the Women's Amendments to the Manhood Suffrage Bill will be discussed and voted upon. This means that within a few short days the fate of these Amendments will be finally decided.

The W.S.P.U. has from the first declined to call any truce on the strength of the Prime Minister's so-called pledge, and has refused to depend upon the Amendments in question, because the Government have not accepted the responsibility of getting them carried. There are, however, some Suffragists—and there may be some even in the ranks of the W.S.P.U.—who hope against hope that in spite of the Government's intrigues an unofficial Amendment may be carried. Feeling as they do, these Suffragists are tempted to hold their hand as far as militancy is concerned, until after the fate of the Amendments is known.

But every member of the W.S.P.U. recognises that the defeat of the Amendments will make militancy more a moral duty and more a political necessity than it has ever been before. We must prepare beforehand to deal with that situation !

There are degrees of militancy. Some women are able to go

further than others in militant action and each woman is the judge of her own duty so far as that is concerned. To be militant in some way or other is, however, a moral obligation. It is a duty which every woman will owe to her own conscience and self-respect, to other women who are less fortunate than she is herself, and to all those who are to come after her.

If any woman refrains from militant protest against the injury done by the Government and the House of Commons to women and to the race, she will share the responsibility for the crime. Submission under such circumstances will be itself a crime.

I know that the defeat of the Amendments will prove to thousands of women that to rely only on peaceful, patient methods, is to court failure, and that militancy is inevitable.

We must, as I have said, prepare to meet the crisis before it arises. Will you therefore tell me (by letter, if it is not possible to do so by word of mouth), that you are ready to take your share in manifesting in a practical manner your indignation at the betrayal of our cause.

Yours sincerely,

(Signed) *E. Pankhurst*

Emmeline Pankhurst writes an open letter to members of the WSPU calling for militant action if government promises to add female suffrage to the Male Suffrage Bill are defeated. The defeat, she says, means 'militancy is inevitable.' The Bill is dismissed in January 1913. *CRIM 1/139/2* part to change the helpless situation in which women find themselves. Flicking through her London guide book for inspiration, Leonora hovers on a page about the Tower of London. She has found the perfect target for attack. Through a stroke of good luck, she enters the Tower with a school group, pretending to be their teacher. But once inside, any pretence of being a law-abiding citizen is immediately abandoned. As she heads to the Crown Jewels, the ultimate symbol of the British government – and their repression of women - she pulls out an iron crow bar she has smuggled in, and smashes the display case. A note attached to the crow bar reads 'This is my protest against the government's treachery to the working women of Great Britain.' She is promptly arrested. She is acquitted only by good fortune: the damage done is less than £5 and means she can't be charged with 'malicious damage.' She returns to Leeds, where she continues to exasperate local police through her militant actions.

The Royal Botanical gardens in Kew, another symbol of the Crown and, by extension, government, suffers a double attack in early 1913. At closing time on one February evening, as the last visitors make their way towards the park gates to leave, Suffragettes are hiding amongst the trees. Under the cover of darkness, they sneak away to the famous orchid houses, and smash the glass panes. They flee, managing to slip away undetected. But, just two weeks later, on 20 February, Lillian Lenton and Olive Wharry sneak into the Gardens in the early hours of the morning and inflict more serious and longer-lasting damage. The two women fling cotton wads soaked with paraffin at the wooden tea pavilion – currently in the process of refurbishment – and set it ablaze. Just 22 minutes later, the only evidence of the existence of tea pavilion is the ashes and debris lying in its place, and, according to some reports, a message: 'good will to all men – when women get the vote'.

The two women flee, racing across the cricket pitches just outside of the Gardens, and, in the process, casting aside the evidence – a hammer, a saw and tow smelling of tar - as they run. This time, the Suffragettes are not as lucky and are caught. They are both sentenced to 18 months' imprisonment and ordered to pay the costs of £400 that are not covered by the insurance. Wharry teeters on apologising to the owners saying she is 'sorry that the two ladies had sustained loss' as she believed it was in the property of the Crown. But, both refuse to pay the costs, explaining – no doubt of no consolation to the owners – that they are at war and even non-combatants must suffer. Despite the sentence and treatment as common criminals, both consider themselves to be 'morally not guilty.' Both are wise enough to know that ill-health can secure release and promptly go on hunger strike.

Other Suffragettes take to less dangerous, but nonetheless equally damaging, attacks on traditionally male-only venues. Numerous golf courses are torn up and Suffragettes

Photographs showing the destruction caused to the tea pavilion in Kew Gardens.'
HO 144/1205/221873/4450i

replace the flags by the holes with flags of their own, bearing the words 'Votes for Women.' Various cricket stands are set alight. Elsewhere, in Moseley, a suburb of Birmingham, local suffragettes fill residents' key holes preventing them from entering their property. No explanation is given other than a leaflet informing them these tactics will stop when 'you demand votes for women and get it.'

The tactics certainly do not stop, and there is an evident escalation of violence. Some women (and men) – often acting on their own initiative - take to planting bombs and chemicals in places to cause maximum physical and symbolic destruction. Corrosives are hidden in letterboxes and in other, sometimes surprising, places for unsuspecting members of the public to make an unpleasant discovery. One innocent man gets more than he bargained for in the toilets at Piccadilly Tube station when he discovers a brown package labelled "nitro-glycerine, dangerous". As the police shrewdly observe, the fact it was discovered in men's toilets make it likely that it was planted by a man. Men, too, though fewer in numbers, also take part in the deliberate campaign of destruction, in protest against the government's stance towards women's suffrage.

One of the most prominent government figures, David Lloyd -George, the Chancellor of the Exchequer, is the next target on the Suffragettes' list. Despite his proclamations of support for women's suffrage, the WSPU feel

In February 1913, Lillian Lenton and Olive Wharry set fire to the tea pavilion in Kew Gardens. The two women are arrested and sentenced to 18 months. They must also pay the cost of the prosecution and pay £100 each. *HO 144/1205/221873*

THE SUFFRAGIST OUTRAGE AT KEW.

SENTENCE ON THE ACCUSED.

IMPRISONMENT AND PAYMENT OF COSTS.

At the Central Criminal Court yesterday, before Mr. Justice Bankes, Olive Wharry, otherwise known as Joyce Locke, 23, student, on bail, was indicted for setting fire to the refreshment pavilion at Kew Gardens. She was found *Guilty* and sentenced to pay the costs of the prosecution, to be imprisoned for 18 months in the second division, and to find two sureties in £100 each to be of good behaviour for two years.

The defendant pleaded " Not Guilty."

Mr. Bodkin and Mr. Travers Humphreys prosecuted for the Director of Public Prosecutions ; Mr. Langdon, K.C., and Mr. R. D. Muir defended.

A number of women were present in Court during the hearing of the case, orders having been given by Mr. Justice Bankes that women should be admitted.

Mr. BODKIN, in opening the case, said the indictment charged the defendant with setting fire to the refreshment pavilion at Kew Gardens on the early morning of February 20. The whole building and contents were destroyed, and upon the two ladies who held the refreshment contract from the Crown a heavy pecuniary loss had been thrown by this act which the prosecution said was clearly the act of the defendant. The building, which was estimated to be worth £900, was insured for £500. At about a quarter-past 3 on the morning of February 20 an employee of Kew Gardens noticed a light in the refreshment pavilion, and saw two forms in the darkness. He gave the alarm and also got out the hose and tried to extinguish the fire. Two policemen named Relf and Hill, noticing a reflection of fire in the sky, ran towards the Gardens and saw the defendant and another woman running away. The officers pursued the women, each of whom threw away a bag or portmanteau. Police-constable Hill ran after the other woman while Relf caught the defendant. The officer told her he should have to take her to the police station, and she rejoined, " Don't hold me ; I will go quietly." One of the portmanteaus contained a saw, hammer, and bundle of tow smelling of tar. On the way to the station the defendant said, " I wonder what the men on duty in the Gardens were doing that they did not see it done." At the police station the other woman gave the name of Lilian Lenton, but she was not before the jury as she was too ill to appear before the justices on the remand day, and they were not now concerned with her. The defendant gave the name of Joyce Locke, but subsequently when applying for bail she gave her true name of Olive Wharry. They were charged with the offence of setting fire to the building and the defendant said " Yes, that is right."

The Chancellor of the Exchequer, David Lloyd George, pictured here, is also targeted. His new house, not yet completed, is damaged by home-made explosives in 1913. Although the suspects are never caught, Emmeline Pankhurst, as leader, takes responsibility and is sentenced to three years' imprisonment. *COPY 1/514/494*

betrayed and outraged by his seeming disingenuousness; his support has, so far, amounted to no reconciliation with the Liberal government. The Suffragettes make their betrayal known. They plant two bombs in his new home. The ropey nature of the home-made explosives means that only one of the bomb detonates, but it is enough to cause £500 worth of damage. Fortunately, for the Suffragettes - and the workmen who discover the second bomb - the other device planted does not detonate. The Suffragettes are never caught, but, thankfully for the police, Emmeline Pankhurst claims responsibility at a meeting in Cardiff a few weeks later. She declares that she is guilty for advising, conspiring and inciting. The police agree, and she is sentenced to three years in prison.

The capital feels the full brunt of the Suffragettes' wrath and bombs are planted in historic sites of importance for the government: the Bank of England, the Coronation Chair at Westminster Abbey and the Bishop's Throne in St Paul's Cathedral are all targeted. Despite the Pankhursts' denial that they intend to harm anyone, it is only good fortune that the unreliable nature of home-made bombs or prompt discovery, that means no civilians are injured. In St Paul's the deacons are conducting services next to the bomb just three hours before it is intended to go off. The plot makes headlines nationally. Although the culprits successfully evade capture (once again), the finger of suspicion naturally points to the WSPU. The only clue the police have to go on is the fact that the bomb was found 'wrapped in brown paper and in part of the recent issue of the militant newspaper The Suffragette.'

Much to the annoyance and embarrassment of the Metropolitan police, dozens of culprits continue to avoid arrest, because, as the police sourly note, they 'have at their disposal two Motor Cars which they use […] in connection with their numerous acts or attempted acts of incendiarism, also for the purpose of escaping arrest.' The police simply cannot keep up with them 'owing to the fact that when outside the town they travel too fast.' The Inspector, desperate not to be outmanoeuvred by Suffragettes any longer, requests a motorbike for one of his officers, Police Sergeant Smith (as the only officer with experience of riding a motorbike), to put on a chase. He estimates the motorbike will cost between £55- £70. The Suffragettes, it seems, are yet again one step ahead, making the most of the latest technology at their disposal from their upper-class members; the government and police can only play catch-up.

For those Suffragettes who do not have a car at their disposal to flee police, a seemingly endless – and dangerous - cycle of hunger striking and force feeding continues. Released Suffragettes continue to relay their ordeal to the press. The public outcry is immense. To limit the reputational damage of the Liberal party, the government hurriedly passes a new act through parliament in April 1913: the Temporary Discharge for Ill Health.

20

CENTRAL OFFICER'S {
SPECIAL REPORT. }

SUBJECT ___ re ___
employment of
motor cyclist.

REFERENCE TO PAPERS.

6000-1 10000-8-13 M.P.

METROPOLITAN POLICE.

CRIMINAL INVESTIGATION DEPARTMENT,

NEW SCOTLAND YARD,

6th. *day of* __ January. __ 191 4.

With reference to the temporary employment of P. S. 14 Smith, Public Carriage Branch, in this Department as a motor cyclist, with the object of covering the movements of militant suffragettes who use motor cars, I beg to report that he has been usefully employed off and on, during the past three months, in locating motor cars used by persons visiting places frequented by suffragettes, and in making enquiries regarding the owners of such cars.

It has been found that the motor cycle he uses for this purpose is of an inferior type, and unable to successfully follow a high power car where the traffic conditions enable it to assume high speed, and therefore, it has not been possible to do full justice to this experiment of attempting to supervise the movements of Suffragettes by a motor cyclist. It is not, for the moment, intended to ask sanction for a continuance of Sergeant Smith's services, and it is recommended

-2-

21

that he might revert to his duty in the Public

Carriage Office, on the completion of the three months

probationary cycle work sanctioned by Home Office.

The tactics of militant Suffragettes using

motor cars in the carrying out of crimes, will be

carefully noted, and if it is found that good results

might be likely to follow the employment of a good

motor cyclist to prevent the execution of their

criminal designs, the Secretary of State might have

to be approached, with a view of again giving sanction

for the employment of a motor cyclist with an up to

date machine.

P. Quinn
Superintendent.

8002-1 10000-4-13 M.P.

This police letter reports on the effectiveness of the one motorcycle requested in order to pursue Suffragettes using cars to flee from their crimes. The report states that the motor cycle 'is of an inferior type' and unable to keep up with the Suffragettes. *MEPO 2/1566*

As soon as the women are deemed too ill – as a result of their hunger-strikes – for imprisonment, they are released. But, after a brief period of recuperation, sometimes of only a few days, they are re-arrested to serve the rest of their sentence. In this way, the government hope to prevent the 'necessity' of force feeding. It also means that a prisoner is less likely to die under the government's watch, therefore avoiding the creation of a martyr for the cause. The cycle usually begins again.

A tirade of WSPU propaganda is once again unleashed. In an attempt to outline the inhumanity of the government and prison doctors who have now 'become a police force', and placing the medical profession in disrepute, they label the act as 'a crime against the human body'. The seemingly unending cycle can be repeated to an extent that 'the health of the Suffragette is completely deranged and until as a final outcome death ensues'. The Suffragette – edited by Christabel Pankhurst – reports on the state of those Suffragette prisoners who have been released under the Act. Her mother, Emmeline

The Suffragette april 11th 1913

STATEMENT BY RELEASED PRISONERS.

News has reached the offices of the W.S.P.U. that Mrs. Pankhurst, who has been hunger-striking ever since she entered Holloway on Thursday, April 3, is in a state of collapse. There has been no attempt to feed her by force.

During the week four Suffragettes have been released from Holloway—Miss Olive Wharry, Miss Gibb, Mrs. Branson, and Miss Zelie Emerson—all on account of serious ill-health. Miss Wharry had been secretly hunger-striking for 31 days, and is in a state of terrible emaciation, and Miss Emerson, after five weeks' forcible feeding, was so dangerously ill that she was taken away from the prison in an ambulance.

Rumours of a hunger-strike that seems as if it it were more or less general have leaked out from Holloway. Indignation and passionate protest are the order of the day inside prison as well as out.

In April 1913, the Government pass a bill to allow for the release of hunger striking prisoners and their re-arrest once they are deemed fit enough to continue their sentence. This follows the public outcry after articles, like this in *The Suffragette*, report on the emaciated condition of five Suffragettes, including Emmeline Pankhurst, after hunger-striking for weeks, and, in some cases, forced feeding.

HO 144/1205/221873

Pankhurst, upon her release from Holloway, is reported as in a state of collapse, whilst Miss Wharry is said to be in state of 'terrible emaciation.'. To the women, it compares to cats playing with their prey just before killing it, and it soon becomes known as the 'Cat and Mouse Act.'

Once again, though, the government underestimates the spirit of the Suffragettes; they are more determined than ever. Many hunger-striking Suffragettes are arrested and re-arrested several times. Partly in response to this Act, the Suffragettes' actions become yet more extreme. There is no telling where, or who, might be targeted next.

On 4 June 1913, Epsom hosts one of the most anticipated and prestigious events of the year: annual Derby Day. Thousands of spectators flock to the course and excitement is brewing. The race itself is proving to be the tensest for years; it is too tight to call a winner as the first horses turn onto the final straight and it is neck and neck as two approach the finish line.

As the King's horse, Anmer – a little behind the rest of the pack – turns onto Tattenham Corner, a tall, red-headed woman subtly, and daringly, slips underneath the railing, undetected by the crowds. She runs straight at Anmer in the middle of the course and flings her arms up in the air. Anmer collides with her. The jockey, Herbert Jones, is thrown off his horse, and the young woman slumps to the ground. Both are unconscious.

Crowds quickly rush to the scene of the collision. Amidst the chaos and confusion, police can identify the woman as Emily Wilding Davison and recognise her immediately as the militant suffragette.

Dr Vale-Jones is one of those who races to her aid, but he finds she is 'suffering from concussion of the brain and heart failure and her life ebbing fast.' She is in a critical condition. He calls 'for brandy or whisky, and a policeman brought [him] the latter, but this had but little effect.' He turns to a nearby nurse and urges her to find some hot water. When there is none to be found, a policeman obtains 'a thermos flask that contained very hot tea […]' Using the nurse's handkerchief, he 'poured some of the contents on and applied it to the left wrist.' Despite Dr Vale-Jones' best efforts, Emily dies four days later, never regaining consciousness.

Publicity for the Suffragettes peaks. Rumours over Emily's intentions spread, and newspapers are rife with contradicting tales. Some witnesses claim that it is a calculated act, a deliberate attempt to sabotage the race and inflict damage on the King's horse – as a symbol of protest against the entire government. Other witnesses claim that she simply thought all the horses had passed, whilst other sources report it merely as an act of lunacy by a mad suffragette, who had every intention to commit suicide. Many seem to be more concerned with the fate of the horse itself.

239,582.

20th June, 1913.

My Lord,

I have the honour, by direction of the Secretary
of State, to say that he has ordered the release under the
Prisoners (Temporary Discharge for Ill-health) Act, 1913,
of Agnes Lake and Laura Geraldine Lennox who were convicted
of conspiracy before your Lordship on the 17th instant
at the Central Criminal Court and sentenced to 6 months'
imprisonment.

Both these prisoners have refused all food since
their reception into Prison and the Law Officers have
advised that in view of the decision of the High Court in the
case of Leigh v. Gladstone the Prison Authorities are precluded
from allowing a prisoner to starve himself to death: and
the only alternative to releasing these prisoners was therefore to feed them forcibly.   Having regard to the fact
that the recent Act was passed by Parliament for the express
purpose of avoiding the necessity for forcibly feeding
prisoners of this class the Secretary of State felt that
he had no option but to release Lake and Lennox temporarily.
By the terms of their discharge they have to return to
Prison at the end of a week and their sentence is suspended
while they are at large.

All the other prisoners who were convicted at
the same time are also refusing their food and Mr. McKenna
fears

The Honourable

Mr. Justice Phillimore,

On circuit,

Maidstone.

PRISONERS (TEMPORARY DISCHARGE FOR ILL-HEALTH) ACT, 1913.

Registered No. and Name of Prisoner - - -	239,582. Agnes Lake.
Court - - - -	Central Criminal Court.
Date of Conviction - -	27 May, 1913.
Offence of which convicted	Conspiracy.
Sentence - - - -	6 months' imprisonment, and find sureties.
Prison in which confined at date of this Order.	Holloway.

Order of the Secretary of State for Temporary Discharge of Prisoner.

Whereas the Prisoner above described is now confined in the above mentioned Prison : and whereas I am satisfied that, by reason of the condition of the said prisoner's health, it is undesirable to detain her in prison, but that, such condition of health being due in whole or part to her own conduct in prison, it is desirable that her release should be temporary and conditional.

I hereby order the temporary discharge of the above described prisoner until the _____ 19th _____ day of _____ December, _____ 1913 subject to the conditions specified below.

Given at Whitehall on the _____ 12th _____ day of _____ December, 1913 .

_____ (sd) R. McKenna. _____

Secretary of State.

To the Governor of H.M. Prison

at _____ Holloway. _____

and all others whom it may concern.

CONDITIONS.

1. The prisoner shall return to the above mentioned Prison on the _____ 19th _____ day of _____ December, _____ 19 13 .

2. The period of temporary discharge granted by this Order may, if the Secretary of State thinks fit, be extended on a representation by the prisoner that the state of her health renders her unfit to return to prison. If such representation be made, the prisoner shall submit herself, if so required, for medical examination by the Medical Officer of the above mentioned Prison or other registered medical practitioner appointed by the Secretary of State.

3. The prisoner shall notify to the Commissioner of the Metropolitan Police the place of residence to which she goes on her discharge. The prisoner shall not change her residence without giving one clear day's previous notice in writing to the Commissioner specifying the residence to which she is going, and she shall not be temporarily absent from her residence for more than twelve hours without giving a like notice.

4. The prisoner shall abstain from any violation of the law.

G.709. 125—4/13. W. & Co., Ltd.
(K5291.) Wt.10947—26. 400.—6/13.   ,,   ,,
(K6218.) 768. 375—9/13.   ,,   ,,

_In_ 33412
564 _BH_

Holloway Prison.

11.12. 1913.

PRISON COMMISSION
1 2 DEC 1913

Daily Report on

4125 _Agnes Lake._

(1) What is the physical and mental condition of the prisoner?

Tongue clean & moist; choreic movements observed on reception more marked today.

(2) Is the prisoner taking food voluntarily? _No_

(3) If not, is the prisoner refusing both (a) food (b) water, and what sorts of food have been offered to the prisoner with a view to inducing a different attitude?

(a) + (b) Yes; various appetising food

(4) General Conduct? _Indifferent_

(5) General Remarks in the case of a prisoner refusing food, particularly as to the physical effect of the refusal, and the length of time that it can be continued without serious risk. Also, whether the prisoner could, if necessary, be fed forcibly?

Had a somewhat sleepless night. No urgent symptoms.

Telephone report 11 a.m. 12th Dec 1913
Has just been discharged. Sent in taxi-cab to home at 65 Wallwood Road, Leytonstone. Took food last night & again this morning. Condition fairly satisfactory on discharge.

Medical Officer.

2.

Submitted.

_12/12/13_

Governor.

(12205 – 17-7-13)

Agnes Lake's sentence of imprisonment was
6 months   or 180 days. It was passed on June 17 1913

As sentences passed during Assizes
are dated from the first day of the
Assizes (in this case May 27) She was
reckoned as having served before Sentence   Days
was passed – – –   –   –   –   –   –   22
    Her first period in prison was –   –   –   4
    " Second "   –   –   –   –   –   –   –   8 3
    " present " " " Since rearrest has been – –   2
                                                    ―――――
                                        Total   111

She has therefore 69 days still to serve, but if she had
earned full marks in prison 30 of these would be remitted

Three days into their sentence, Agnes Lake and Laura Geraldine Lennox are released under the 'Cat and Mouse Act.' Agnes is released again in December 1913, with 69 days left to serve on her sentence. *HO 144/1275/239582*

New No. 728.
Old No. 6.

Reference to Papers.

Corres

770809

Metropolitan Police.

Lee Road STATION.   R   DIVISION.

5th June 1913

With reference to attached Correspondence. I beg to report that at about 3pm on 4th inst I was on duty on Epsom Race Course when the race for the Derby Stakes took place.

When the horses were rounding Tattenham Corner, Miss Emily Davison, a well known militant Suffragette suddenly rushed from under the rail immediately in front of "Anmer" a horse owned by H.M. The King, and ridden by Herbert Jones.

The woman was knocked down and rendered unconscious, the horse was thrown down and the jockey also rendered unconscious.

Police of "N" Division were on duty at the spot and P.S. 4th Bunn 8th Burridge and P.C. 59th Eady promptly went to the assistance of the woman, and Insp. Whitbread "N" with P.C. 59th Brown, 8th Phillips and 85th Johnson attended to the

This police report describes events at Epsom Derby. Police claim that Emily 'suddenly rushed from under the rail' in front of Anmer, the King's horse. Conflicting versions over Emily's intentions spread. Some argue it was an act of sabotage, whilst others believe she intended to commit suicide.

MEPO 2/1551

In this photo, Emily is visible on the floor unconscious. The collision also knocks down Anmer, one of the King's horse, and flings the jockey, Herbert Jones, off. They, too, are visible in the photograph. *ZPER 34/142*

Emily herself argued the need for a 'great tragedy' – a martyr for the cause. She had previously thrown herself down the stairs at Holloway to rebel against what she described as the torture of force feeding. However, since the police discover a return ticket to Victoria station and two WSPU flags on her body, some reports believe it is possible she simply wanted to attach the Suffragette flag on to the King's course as a symbolic act of rebellion.

Although witness statements and reports all seem to contradict her intentions, the WSPU does not pass up on the opportunity to use her funeral to generate yet more publicity. Thousands line the street – some to pay their respects; other, no doubt, out of morbid curiosity. Whether or not Emily intended to become a martyr, she becomes one.

Emily's actions only seem to spur on some militants, who vow to continue the fight whatever the cost – to themselves or the nation. Knowing that a destruction of the nation's

Thousands line the street for the funeral of Emily Wilding Davison on Saturday 14th June 1913. Thousands of Suffragettes, led by Emmeline Pankhurst, wearing white, with a black armband and carrying white lilies follow her coffin through the streets of central London. *ZPER 34/142*

culture and history will provoke an outcry (making it harder to ignore their cause), several Suffragettes continue deliberately to damage valuable pieces of artwork in galleries across the nation.

Manchester Art Gallery is one of the first to be targeted by suffragettes in the North-West of England. In April 1913, Annie Briggs, Lillian Forrester and Evelyn Manesta, members of the WSPU, pass themselves off as three 'normal' visitors, enjoying the finest artworks Manchester has to offer. But, just as the Gallery is due to close, they take out a hammer they have managed to conceal and run amok, smashing the display cases surrounding the artworks. In the struggle for arrest, the hammer is dropped and the WSPU colours, purple, green and white, can be seen attached to it, along with a message: 'parliament for dishonourable men, prison for honourable women.' Their justification for the damages is clear. The police are issued with specific instructions upon Lilly and Evelyn's release from prison, fearing that they 'may endeavour to perpetrate similar outrages.' Descriptions of the two women are circulated so that they may be easily identified.

Whilst Lilly and Evelyn are under surveillance, they don't commit any more damage towards artworks, but, various other Suffragettes, working alone or in small groups, are inspired.

The Victoria and Albert Museum, the British Museum and the Wallace Collection are prime targets in the capital. The women know that destruction of these collections, some of the most valuable historic and art collections of the nation, will cause maximum devastation and therefore have the biggest impact. Mary Richardson, on temporary release from prison, is aware of this, and targets one of the National Gallery's most prized paintings, Valasquez's Rokeby Venus in March 1914. As she pulls out a meat cleaver and begins to hack away at the painting, she is restrained by a guard, but not before considerable damage has been inflicted. She is sentenced to six months in prison, and earns the nickname in the press of 'Slasher Mary', in reference to the multiple slashes made to the painting. The damage is considerable. The restoration costs are estimated at £100; the devaluation of the painting at £10,000.

The lengthy prison sentences do not dissuade Suffragettes from committing further acts of vandalism in galleries and museums up and down the country. Museums in Edinburgh, Surrey and Birmingham experience extensive damages to their collections by fervent Suffragettes. Bertha Ryland, lingering near the famous 'Master Thornhill' painting in Birmingham Art Gallery in June 1914, suddenly pulls out a concealed chopper and 'strikes three downward blows' at the picture. She is arrested and charged with 'malicious damage.' Her defence team try to argue her 'hysterical condition' to diminish her responsibility of her actions, but Bertha herself refutes this defence. In a statement made to police she claims it was a deliberate 'protest against the government's criminal injustice in denying women the vote.' This is not her first offence. She is sentenced to 6 months imprisonment in 1912 for breaking windows to the value of £6 (and £1 over the threshold for malicious damage). The severity of the sentence infuriates her brother who writes an angry letter to the Home Office, comparing it to the case of a man who is sentenced to just one month for causing £100 worth of damage to windows. 'Is this British justice?' he asks.

Following this spate of attacks, museum directors, particularly in London museums, fear for the safety of their collections. The National Gallery, the Wallace Collection and the Tate Gallery temporarily close, and emergency talks are held. Museum directors discuss the erection of glass screens to shield the paintings from further Suffragette damage, and women – not just known Suffragettes - must from now on leave bags in the cloakroom.

221863/22

J. ERNEST HILL,
PROSECUTING SOLICITOR FOR
THE CITY.

TELEPHONE CENTRAL 5972.

VICTORIA COURTS,

BIRMINGHAM.

25th September 1914.

Sir,

Rex v. Bertha Ryland.

This prisoner was charged at the Midsummer Sessions
this year with wilful damage to a picture called "Master
Thornhill" by Romney, on the 9th June 1914, the said picture
at that time being in the Birmingham Art Gallery open to the
public.

The facts of the case are these. The defendant was a
militant Suffragette. On the 9th June she went to the Art
Gallery and was there seen by an attendant to pull a chopper
from under her jacket and strike three downward blows at the
picture. The damage amounted to about £50. Near the
picture was found a paper on which was written in the
defendant's handwriting, a statement a copy of which is sent
herewith. At the Sessions the prisoner was unable to
appear and evidence was given to that effect by Dr. Beatrice
Webb of Birmingham, who said it would be dangerous for the
defendant to plead. The case was accordingly remitted to
the ensuing Assizes in July of this year.

On that occasion a further certificate of Dr. Beatrice
Webb was sent to me by the defendant's father, but I declined
to accept Dr. Webb's evidence and asked for the evidence of
Dr. Billington, a women's doctor in Birmingham who would not
be likely to have any sympathy with the position taken up
by the suffrage movement. Dr. Billington gave evidence that
the defendant was unable to appear/that she would be operated
on for kidneys. The case was accordingly remitted to the
next Assizes.

J. ERNEST HILL,
PROSECUTING SOLICITOR FOR
THE CITY.

TELEPHONE CENTRAL 5972.

VICTORIA COURTS,

BIRMINGHAM.

2.

In view of the present position I shall be glad if you
will inform me whether you think it is advisable for the
prosecution to offer any evidence at the next Assizes. From
information that has come to my knowledge and from a private
statement made to me by Dr. Billington, I think it is quite
possible that the defendant's mind was more or less affected
at the time she committed the offence with which she is charged
and although I think she was responsible for her actions
there is no doubt that she was in an hysterical condition which
might possibly have made her more than ordinarily liable to do
such an act of damage.

I understand also that at the present time the militant
suffrage movement has declared an "Armistice" and it occurs
to me that it may be you would desire that nothing should
be done which might in any way affect the present quiet of
the society. I believe that the defendant would be willing
to apologise for the damage she has done and give an undertaking not to do any further damage. She has just undergone
an operation from which she has not recovered and I think
it may be that if she is treated leniently and an undertaking
is obtained from her, she will not offend again.

I shall be obliged if you will let me hear from you
and if you think that some such action as I suggest ought to
be taken perhaps you will like me to approach the defendant
and her people without prejudice and obtain from them a
statement as to what they are prepared to do.

It may be also that you will think that if the case
is to be withdrawn, the defendant should make some

These letters from the solicitors to the Home Office describe the case of Bertha Ryland, who attacks the 'Master Thornhill' painting with an axe. The prosecution ask for leniency for her sentence due to her 'hysterical condition' – although Berta rejects this line of defence. *HO 144/1205/221862*

Copy Exhibit "A",
    I.

Christ says "I came not to bring Peace but a Sword".

I attack this work of art deliberately, as a protest against the Government's criminal injustice in denying women the vote and also against the Government's brutal injustice in imprisoning, forcibly feeding and drugging Suffragist militants while allowing Ulster militants to go free.

Let all sensible men and women enquire into the cause of militancy instead of condemning the militants. We are militant because only so can the Vote be won; we need the Vote because only by it can the Woman's Movement become a truly effective power. The Woman's Movement means the spiritual, mental and physical salvation of the race, because it is the one Movement that undertakes to stamp out sexual immorality and all its attendant horrors.

It is futile to attempt to crush this great Movement by persecution and misrepresentation. No power on earth can stop a Movement that is working, with Divine Guidance, for Purity and Righteousness.

                    BERTHA RYLAND.

This is a typed copy of a letter left by Berta Ryland after damaging the painting. She writes that she attacked the work deliberately 'in protest against the Government's brutal injustice' towards Suffragettes.

HO 144/1205/221862

3020, Mayfair.

REFERENCE 34/14

*Any reply to this letter
should be addressed to—*

THE KEEPER.

Copy.

TRUSTEES OF THE WALLACE COLLECTION,

Hertford House,

Manchester Square, W.

19th March 1914.

Sir,

At a meeting of the Trustees held this morning to discuss measures of precaution in view of the recent suffragist
outrage at the National Gallery, they decided that it is essen-
tial to the protection of the Collection that two detectives
familiar with the appearance of the women chiefly concerned
should be stationed in the Entrance Hall with instructions to
exclude all suspicious characters. They considered further
that if this step were taken the two Constables in plain clothes
at present patrolling the Galleries might be dispensed with.

It is only on these terms that the Trustees can see
their way to a partial reopening of the Collection. I am
therefore to ask that authority for the slight extra expense
may be granted, this expense during the ensuing financial year
to be met out of savings on the Vote generally.

It is the desire of the Trustees to reopen the Gallery
on Monday next the 23rd instant. May I therefore ask for a
reply at your very earliest convenience.

I am, Sir,

Your obedient Servant,

(So) D.S.Macboll,

The Secretary,
    H.M.Treasury,   S.W.

Museums fear for
their collections after
a spate of vandalism
in national museums.
The National
Gallery decides it is
necessary to place
two plain clothed
detectives at the
entrance to prevent
any 'suspicious
characters.'
© *The Wallace Collection
AR 1/39*

The National Gallery, upon its reopening, requests two detectives to guard the entrance and 'exclude all suspicious characters.' The Treasury agrees to fund this, and two detectives are put in place for a period of six months. The British Museum refuses to admit women without an acknowledgement that someone is responsible for their behaviour, or unless they are in the company of a man. Women everywhere are being treated as potential militants.

At the height of Suffragette militancy in March 1914, the government continue to arrest WSPU members. But it is the WSPU's leadership – the Pankhursts, Pethwick -Lawrences and Annie Kenney in particular – who the police are most keen to arrest, perhaps hoping that, without any leadership, the WSPU will fade into obscurity. The leadership are placed under careful police surveillance, their movements tracked. Officers and journalists, working for the government, are planted in meetings, disguised as advocates for the cause, or hidden, observing from afar. They are ordered to keep detailed transcripts of the proceedings, and to collect pamphlets, adverts and publications for the use of possible evidence. The police are hoping to be able to catch them red-handed, inciting and encouraging violence, allowing them to legally arrest the leading Suffragettes.

One WSPU meeting at Knightsbridge Hall is infiltrated by Mr Champion, a journalist working for the Press Association. His notes are meticulous and, ironically, some of the best minutes of the meeting's proceedings. During the opening speech, Mrs Dacre-Fox, General Secretary of the movement, reads a message from Mrs Pankhurst who is still recovering from her latest hunger strike in prison after her re-arrest in Glasgow. Mr Champion notes the exact message, in which Mrs Pankhurst informs the audience that she 'rejoices in the courage of women and the splendid example they are giving to the world in …the achievement of a great purpose.' She adds, as noted by Champion, that 'the government and the Nation must be made to understand that militancy can only be brought to an end… by doing them justice.' Champion notes the cheers given by the audience when individual militant acts are mentioned, particularly Miss Mary Richardson ('Slasher Mary'), who Mrs Dacre-Fox, claims to be 'one of the most amazing women of the age.' The meeting celebrates women's achievements to date, and aims to keep up morale and maintain the spirits of those beginning to doubt the effectiveness of militancy. It is a cry to continue battle: 'The government have got to give us the vote, or, as Mrs Pankhurst is reported to have said, "they have got to kill us."'

As well as short hand transcripts of the meetings, secret photographs of members are taken for future identification in a bid to clamp down on their violence.

Gaol provides the perfect opportunity for taking photographs of known militant Suffragettes. At first, this involves taking mug shots of Suffragettes upon arrival as has been procedure for convicted criminals since 1891. The Suffragettes, again outraged that they

KEY TO ABOVE PHOTOGRAPHS OF KNOWN MILITANT SUFFRAGETTES.

Fig.	Name.	Year born	Height Ft. In.	Eyes	Hair.	C.R.O. Number	Crime.
1	Scott Margaret	1888	5. 3	Blue.	D.Brown.	S.168279	Damage.
2	Hookin Olive.	1881	5. 3½	Brown	Brown	S.169280	Conspiry.
3	McFarlane Margaret	1888	5. 1	Hazel	Brown	S.168518	Damage
4	Wyan Mary @ Nellie Taylor.	1864	5. 1	Brown	Brown	S.168705	Damage
5	Bell Annie @ Hannah Booth and Elizabeth Bell.	1874	5.6½	Blue	Lt.Brn.	S.165769	Damage
6	Short Jane @ Rachel Peace.	1882	5. 3	Blue	Brown	S.168517	Arson
7	Ansell Gertrude Mary	-	5. 4	Grey	Tg.Grey	S.169570	Damage
8	Brindley Maud	1866	5. 3	Grey	Grey	S.167057	Damage
9	Oates Verity	--	5. 0	Brown	Brown	S.172313	Damage
10	Manesta Evelyn	1888	5. 2	Grey	Fair	S.166692	Damage

Covert photographs, like these, are taken of militant suffragettes whilst they are imprisoned. They are accompanied with a 'key' which includes their birth year, height, eye colour, hair colour and their crime. These are issued to police to prevent future crimes or for their re-arrest. *AR 1/528*

are being treated as criminals, once more find a way to rebel. They deliberately move at the last moment so that the photo blurs and is unusable as identification, or deliberately refuse to look at the camera. On occasion, they put up such a struggle that they are forcibly restrained by a prison guard.

As this method is proving increasingly difficult with women deliberately refusing to have their photograph taken, prison warders and police adopt covert photography instead. They take photos of Suffragettes without their knowledge and frequently from a distance. This is done to varying degrees of success: some are too far away; others are not looking anywhere in the vague direction of the camera, and other women are pulling faces, rendering most of the photographs as useless.

In a final effort both to ensure a satisfactory photograph, but perhaps also as their resistance towards the Suffragettes, they even occasionally resort to force. Evelyn Manesta

Evelyn Manesta resists all police efforts to take her picture whilst in prison. In the end, a police officer must forcefully keep Evelyn still. In the photograph to be used for police memoranda though, the police officer standing behind Evelyn has been removed. *AR1/528*

puts up such a struggle that a policeman puts his hands around her neck to force her to look at the camera (but ensuring he stays deliberately obscured behind her). She still finds a way to ruin the photo and pulls a face at the last moment.

Tellingly, when this photo is later used in a police memorandum for her re-arrest after she attacks public display cases in Manchester Art Gallery, it shows no signs of the policeman at all; it has been doctored, probably to spare the police the humiliation of having forcibly to restrain a woman.

Still, the Suffragettes are showing no sign of slowing down their campaign, and many members of the public express genuine concern and fear over, not only the consequences of women's suffrage, but the means Suffragettes are employing to gain the vote. Newspapers are flooded with letters from the public relating to the actions of 'misguided women', whose controversial methods divide public opinion, with many generally believing their actions are ruinous to the cause.

CRIMINAL RECORD OFFICE,

NEW SCOTLAND YARD, S.W.

24th April, 1914.

MEMORANDUM.

Special attention is drawn to the undermentioned SUFFRAGETTES, who have committed damage to public art treasures, and who may at any time again endeavour to perpetrate similar outrages.

Lillian Forrester (S/167641), age 33, height 5ft. 3½in., complexion pale, hair brown, eyes grey.

Has been convicted of damaging, with a hammer, pictures in the Manchester Art Gallery, and in London of breaking windows.

LILLIAN FORRESTER.   EVELYN MANESTA.

Evelyn Manesta (S/166692), age 26, height 5ft. 2in., complexion pale, hair fair, eyes grey.

Was convicted with Lillian Forrester of damaging, with a hammer, pictures in the Manchester Art Gallery.

Some of the public voice their fear directly to government departments and the police, who receive dozens of letters daily, calling for more direct action to prevent civil unrest, or to inform them of the latest Suffragette plan; the public are becoming their eyes and ears.

Fearing that the police are unaware of the plans for an 'oar parade' in April 1914, a Mrs Highfields takes it upon herself to request extra police presence in Hyde Park. Incredulous to their audacity, she describes how the Suffragettes 'will have all of the boats on the Serpentine' in Hyde Park, and 'if the public should demand any, they will have to hire them of the Suffragettes!' As she explains to the police – who undoubtedly share the same opinion – she fears that 'damages may be in view.' Irrespective of whether Mrs Highfields is a supporter of the cause in principle, she is clearly concerned about public disorder and safety.

Even some members of the WSPU fear that the militant tactics are going too far. Sylvia Pankhurst is beginning to voice objections, and, in 1911, Adela Pankhurst, who, until then, played an active part in heckling ministers' speeches and addressing WSPU meetings, left the WSPU. But, for Emmeline and Christabel – and thousands of their followers – militancy remains the only viable option.

CHAPTER 4

RISING FRUSTRATIONS IN OTHER SUFFRAGE ORGANISATIONS

Although it is the WSPU's extreme tactics that are preoccupying the government and monopolising the attention of the public and the press, other suffrage organisations continue actively, but less destructively, to fight for the cause. Many of these suffrage organisations agree with the government on one thing: militant tactics are outrageous and irresponsible, and are doing more harm than good to women's demands for the vote.

The death of Emily Wilding Davison gains a lot of public sympathy, but is considered by others a new low in Suffragette stunts The 'stunt' is heavily criticised by the NUWSS, who are keen to reclaim the moral high ground and undo some of the damage caused to the suffrage movement in public opinion.

The NUWSS is still the biggest single suffrage organisation – boasting approximately 50,000 members across 449 societies in ten federations by 1913. The WSPU, by comparison, peaks at no more than 5000 members. In a bid to remind the government how many women want the vote, the NUWSS calls upon its members in all parts of the country to join a peaceful 'pilgrimage' to London.

Advertisements are placed in newspapers and posters are distributed to encourage women to participate. In a display of unity, routes are planned so that local branches will join others in their federation along a specific route. The branches and federations will collectively cover the entirety of the country, along eight routes, stretching right from Land's End to John O'Groats.

The NUWSS leadership are not disappointed with the response; women turn out in their tens of thousands. On 18 June 1913, just days after Emily Wilding Davison's funeral, the first women set out on their prescribed march, by bicycle foot or by car (provided by upper class members, who frequently pick up exhausted members en route). Members are instructed to wear only white, black, grey or navy blouses, skirts and hat in a further act of cross-class solidarity. Most are sporting sashes of red, white and green - the colours of the NUWSS.

Along the way, meetings are held to ensure that no part of Britain can escape the meaning of women's suffrage or remain ignorant or indifferent to women's rights.

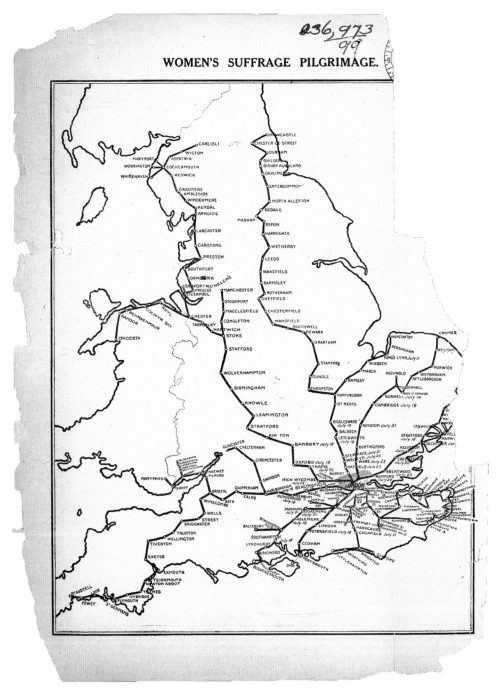

This map shows the eight different routes to bring thousands of members from the NUWSS from across the country for a rally in Hyde Park. Meetings are held along the routes to promote the peaceful fight for women's suffrage. *HO 45/10701/236973*

As at many suffrage demonstrations, the National League for Opposing Women's Suffrage, an amalgamation of the Women's Anti-Suffrage League and the Men's Anti-Suffrage League, offers counter-meetings to the NUWSS, wanting to expose the societal subversion should women be allowed to vote.

They hold over 70 meetings in the same villages and towns that the NUWSS pass through, Women's suffrage, they argue, goes against nature and the natural positions of men and women in society. The President of the Women's National Anti-Suffrage League Mrs Mary Ward, deliberately goes by the name of Mrs Humphrey Ward in public to serve as a reminder of a woman's 'natural' position in relation to her husband i.e. that a woman becomes the man's 'property'. Most women, they counter, do not want the vote at all. This resonates with many women – and men. The National League has more members than the NUWSS and WSPU combined, and huge crowds congregate to listen.

Because of their dominant presence, the NUWSS accuse them of cajoling local residents to threaten the NUWSS speakers and supporters. In Chester, some drunken men are 'quietly removed', and in Nantwich, a small group of children chase the pilgrims with 'dirt and stones.' More serious disturbances are seen in Hanley, Staffordshire, where police note that 'pilgrims are very roughly handled by crowds' after the meeting, and in Newark 'missiles were thrown and one of the platforms rushed.'

The National League is outraged by this allegation and demand a deputation with the Secretary of State, Reginald McKenna, to prove that they 'are not responsible for organising any disorder.' In fact, they persist, 'in many cases they appealed for a fair hearing for "pilgrims."'

Most places, though, see quiet, peaceful meetings go ahead as planned. On 29 July, as the last women reach London, over 50,000 women congregate in Hyde Park in a bid to show the massive volume of support for women's suffrage. The display of calm and dignity – in stark contrast to recent WSPU tactics – is not lost on the government. Asquith, in an unprecedented act of near cooperation, accepts a deputation of NUWSS women. The pilgrimage is a tremendous success.

Amidst the mood of paranoia and anxiety due to militant tactics, and to distance their own groups from the violence, other societies also continue to hold peaceful meetings and seek diplomatic resolutions with the government.

Simultaneous to the pilgrimage and WSPU militancy, the Women's Tax Resistance League make a desperate (passive although not strictly constitutional) effort to make the government see the irrationality behind inequality towards women. On 10 June 1913, seven prominent members of the WFL manage, after several attempts, to seek a deputation with Lloyd George, who has a complicated and slightly thorny relationship with the Women's Suffrage movement. The women do not hold back in voicing their anger at the current societal position of women, in particular of married women and those women paying taxes.

Although legally allowed to earn a separate income, for the purposes of taxation, they point out, a woman's income is merged with her husband's, meaning a higher level of taxation. This, they argue, is an unfair 'tax upon marriage'. Although they are disgruntled by the legal implications of this, meaning a husband may have to pay for his wife's tax, it is the moral unfairness which is most unsatisfactory to the women. Miss Lena Ashwell is outraged when she remarks that she receives a tax bill addressed to a 'Mr H J F Simson and in brackets 'for wife' – despite the fact that she owns and manages the theatre, not her husband. She argues 'if I am not a person but an appendage, it should be impossible for [her] to be on the list of taxpayers'. Another member remarks on the fact that her husband was imprisoned for 15 days for refusing to pay taxes on money which was not his, but her own!

The women therefore threaten to refuse to pay any further taxes on the 'unjust encroachment of the rights of citizens'. Lloyd-George does nothing more than lend a sympathetic ear and he does little to improve his relationship to the women's movement.

Elsewhere, other suffrage organisations continue to protest. The Actresses' Franchise League (AFL), founded in 1908, holds several meetings and plays – many of which are written by the Women Writer's Suffrage League - to outline the injustice of sexual inequality. By 1913, most of the nation's celebrated actresses and comediennes of the day are members, and tour the country with plays and comedies at meetings led by other suffrage organisations. Having watched both militant and peaceful events unfold with still no results, the AFL holds a mass meeting at Drury Lane Theatre. The opening speech, by Lady Willoughby De Broke, calls upon the Prime Minister to 'remove his personal veto and fulfil his pledge' from November 1911, when he led women's suffrage societies to believe that their cause would be discussed in parliament only to reverse his decision. This, she declares, is the only way to prevent the 'present deplorable state of disorder and [see] the women of the country enfranchised'. The WSPU, it seems, are not the only ones feeling betrayed by Asquith's empty promises. The AFL, however, did not officially endorse militant protest campaigns (though some of its members are also members of the WSPU).

Militancy is beginning to have a detrimental impact on other suffrage organisations. On accounts of 'recent rowdyism', the New Constitutional Society for Women's Suffrage and the Men's League for Women's Suffrage, encounter difficulties from officials when attempting to meet in Hyde Park. The Men's League are refused permission for a van and a portable platform, whilst the police eject a well-known speaker of the New Constitutional Society, Mrs Meyers, from the park. The WSPU militancy has clearly unsettled the government enough for it to fear disorder from all suffrage societies – regardless of their nature and stance.

The societies, in turn, seem to be growing increasingly frustrated at both militancy, and the government's response to it. The Men's League inform the Home Office that they will continue their meetings anyway and offer any opposition should the police ask them to close it and the New Constitutional Society lodge a complaint against the treatment by police. The police, Mrs Meyers claims, pushed her and 'hustled her to the park gates' with orders given not to 'let her back again' simply for talking 'in low tones' to a small group of people. This she claims, amounts to spying on the public. She fears the implications on 'the liberty of the subject':

She is not the only one to air these concerns. After WSPU meetings are banned altogether from Hyde Park, the Free Speech Defence Committee is forced into action, and writes to the Secretary of State. It declares that the government's recent antics go 'against the whole spirit of any government that can call itself Liberal.' Furthermore, it argues, police and officials have no right to dictate what is to be tolerated, and, suppression of public meetings will lead to movements moving underground and 'make them more dangerous.'

Women's suffrage, it seems, is at breaking point; neither violent nor peaceful tactics seem to be making any headway for the cause. Neither the WSPU nor the government seems to be satisfying anyone.

The public, government and suffrage societies themselves are growing increasingly exasperated at the situation. Supporters are more desperate than ever for the vote; opponents want a return to normality and 'natural' society. All want an end to the conflict.

On 4 August 1914, the war for suffrage temporarily ends abruptly. Britain must now fight another war.

CHAPTER 5

A NEW WAR

Days after war is declared, the NUWSS announces that it will not protest for women's suffrage for the war's duration. Instead Millicent Fawcett will plead with members to do their duty for the country –to the discontent of many thousands of its members who are pacifists. To the government's relief, the WSPU follows suit.

In the spirit of unity and pulling together, the government declares an amnesty in exchange for a cessation of militant activities. They will release all prisoners still imprisoned, and exonerate those who are released under the Cat and Mouse Act but who have time left to serve. Both sides agree; there is a more pressing war to fight. Emmeline and Christabel Pankhurst, having fled to France to evade imprisonment, return to Britain and order WSPU members to refrain from militancy and instead to play their part for the war effort.

The government fulfils its promise. Instructions are issued to prisons up and down the country to release any prisoners who have been arrested since 1906 in relation to Suffrage activities. It is a bigger undertaking than perhaps initially anticipated. Thousands of women have been prepared to sacrifice their freedom for their principles, often on numerous occasions. In some instances, like Annie Kenney, previous convictions stretch to dozens.

Working from an official list of over 1,300 women and 100 men, hundreds of women and men are released from gaols everywhere, including Birmingham, Manchester, Liverpool, Glasgow and Dublin, as well as smaller towns such as Oldham, Crewe and Croydon. WSPU leaders have relied heavily on its 'foot soldiers' to cause chaos up and down the country from all echelons of society, who have worked together for the same cause; from Princess Sophia Duleep-Singh, the one-time Indian princess now fighting for British women's suffrage, to Minnie Baldock, who set up the Canning Town branch of the WSPU to recruit more working women to the cause. It has been a mass movement of women and men across Britain.

For now though, under orders from Mrs Pankhurst, these women and men are putting their militant methods on hold. Many of the men must enlist and go to the Front, and some of the women voluntarily take up war work, entering factories, becoming nurses, tram conductors and, for the first time ever, police officers, albeit with limited powers. The

Page. Mrs.
  Bow. St. 9/4/09   180,782/6

Page. Robert or
  Robson Paige
    Marlboro' St. 15/7/13   240,691
    Bow. St. 22/5/14   "

Paget. Kathleen.
  Bow St. 11/3/13   /   235,542

Paige. Robson or
  Robert Page
    Marlboro St. 15/7/13   240691
    Bow St. 22/5/14   240,691

Palethorpe, Fanny D. or
Paillthorpe, Fannie Dixon]
    Westminster 4/3/12   220,196/16
    London Sessions 19/3/12   222,056

Palmer, Marguerite
  Bow St. 28/11/11   203,651

Palmer. William. James
  Bow. St. 28/4/13   /   243,950

Pankhurst. Adela E. M.
  Westminster 24/10/06   145,641/1
  Glasgow 21/8/09   182785/1

Pankhurst. Christabel
  Westminster 14/2/07   149,245/2
  Bow St. 14/10/08   170808/3
  Personal file   238,466

Pankhurst. Emmeline
  Westminster 14/2/08   161,505
  Bow St. 14/10/08   170808 805/4
           9/7/09   180,783 546
           2/3/12   220,196/16
  c. c. c. 22/5/12   223,849
  Empson 26/2/13   /   193.784 234,646
  C. C. C 8/4/13   /   "
    also ―   203657
                                   117 118 119 120

Pankhurst. Estelle. Sylvia
  Westminster 24/10/06   145,641/1

Pankhurst. Sylvia
  Westminster 14/2/07   149,245
  Bow St. 29/1/13   234,198
  Thames 14/2/13   "
      "   18/2/13   "
  Bow St. 8/4/13   "
      "   28/4/13   "
      "   2/5/19   "
  Mansion House 23/10/20   414,256]

Parker. Fannie
  Westminster 14/2/08   161,505/20
  W. London 4/3/12   220,196/16
  London Sessions 19/3/12   222,029

Pascoe. Jane
  Bow St. 2/3/12   220,196/16

Pascoe. Mary
  Bow St. 28/4/13 ―   241,292

Paterson. Margaret
  @ Phillips
    Marlboro' St. 7/10/13 /   243,561
    Bow. St.   9/3/13   "
       "   23/3/13 /   "

Paul. Alice
  Bow St. 9/7/09   180,782/6
  Thames 31/7/09   182,086/1
  Guildhall 10/4/09   185,589
  Glasgow 21/8/09   182,785/1

Paul. B. J.
  Bow St. 9/7/09   180,782/6

Payne. Frederick George
  Bow St. 14/10/08   170,808/3

P

After the outbreak of the First World War, the government issues an amnesty to all those suffragettes still in prison. This list records over 1000 suffragettes – men and women – to whom the government are providing amnesty. *HO 45/24665* fight for women's rights does not come to a complete standstill however. The WSPU and WFL continue to pressure the government on specific injustices to women as and when they arise. The Independent WSPU, a break-away branch of the WSPU, forms in 1916 and continues the fight for women's suffrage.

Two months into the war, Nina Boyle, head of the political and militant division of the WFL, becomes aware of recent controversies surrounding women's attendance in court. She calls out for women to let her know of their experiences so that she may contact the Home Office and demand a response. Despite the illegality of excluding women from courtrooms, she receives numerous responses where the judge has taken it upon himself to banish women from the audience. One woman, who remains anonymous, is particularly aggrieved that she was ordered out of a hearing in Ipswich during the case of extra-marital and under-age sexual relations of a 14-year-old girl with a 21-year-old man. A Superintendent ordered her out in 'a most insolent manner' brandishing orders that 'no females were to be allowed in'. She left due to his 'very unpleasant frame of mind'. This is not an isolated case. In 1912, Mary Blake was charged and fined £5 for behaviour 'likely to provoke a breach of the peace'. The alleged breach of the peace was returning immediately after having been ordered out of the courtroom due the 'indecent nature' of the case. She then refused to leave.

After being informed of these cases, Nina Boyle expresses her outrage on behalf of these women. She writes a letter of protest to the Home Office against women 'being so constantly persecuted' in this manner even though they are doing an immense amount of voluntary work for their country. Moreover, it is, she claims, their legal right to attend trials and their exclusion represents an 'attack on their rights and liberties'. The Home Office investigate. But, as before, the male judges defend their actions as protecting women against 'the nature of the evidence' – despite women proving themselves quite capable in men's jobs given their absence.

Similarly, when the governments add Regulation 40d to the Defence of the Realm Act, introduced in August 1914 to protect the nation during war and keep up their morale, the Independent WFL makes its feelings known. The addition of Regulation 40d in early 1918 to the ever-growing impositions on individual liberties, is almost identical to the Contagious Disease Act of 1864, and specifies that any woman who sleeps with a serving soldier can be arrested, and then examined for venereal disease. If she refuses, she will be charged and could be imprisoned for up to six months. There are no repercussions for a serving soldier who passes venereal disease onto a woman.

The government sees the regulation as protection of the forces, particularly from prostitution. But the Independent WFL and WSPU are livid at the blatant sexual double standard, and are fearful that this undoes the progress made by Josephine Butler in her campaign to repeal the Contagious Disease Act for the same reasons. The Regulation

JOINT PROTEST MEETING

AGAINST

REG. 40 D, D.O.R.A.,

AT THE

QUEEN'S HALL,

(Sole Lessees—Messrs. CHAPPELL & Co., Ltd.)

WEDNESDAY, NOVEMBER 6th, at 7.30

(With the co-operation of all the principal Religious & Social Associations.) *See List overleaf.*

The following Resolution will be submitted:—" This Meeting demands the immediate withdrawal of Regulation 40 D under the Defence of the Realm Act."

SPEAKERS:

Mrs. BRAMWELL BOOTH.

Miss MAUDE ROYDEN.

Miss MARY MACARTHUR.

Mr. E. B. TURNER, F.R.C.S.

The Rt. Rev. The LORD BISHOP OF KENSINGTON.

The Rt. Rev. Mgr. PROVOST BROWN (Vicar-Gen., Southwark).

Mrs. HENRY FAWCETT in the Chair.

Reserved Seats, 2s. 6d. & 1s. Admission Free by Ticket, to be obtained from the Secretary of the Association for Moral and Social Hygiene, 19, Tothill Street, S.W. 1, or any of the co-operating Societies.

VACHER & SONS, Ltd., Westminster House, S.W. 1.—66060.

The following Societies have already consented to co-operate in the Joint Protest Meeting against Regulation 40 D, D.O.R.A., at the Queen's Hall, November 6th, 1918, at 7.30 p.m.

Alliance of Honour.
Association of Moral and Social Hygiene.
Baptist Women's League.
Catholic Social Guild.
Catholic Women's Suffrage Society.
Church League for Women's Suffrage.
Committee for Social Investigation and Reform.
Fabian Women's Group.
Free Church League for Women Suffrage.
Friends' Social Purity Association.
Independent Women's Social and Political Union.
London Congregational Union Women's League.
London Society for Women's Suffrage.
Mothers' Union.
National Adult School Union (Women's Committee).
National Amalgamated Union of Shop Assistants.
National British Women's Temperance Association.
National Council for Civil Liberties.
National Organization of Girls' Clubs.
National Political League.
National Union of Women's Suffrage Societies.
National Union of Trained Nurses.
National Union of Teachers.
National Union of Women Workers (London Branch).
Oxford Vigilance Committee.
Penal Reform League.
Primitive Methodist Missionary Society.
Salvation Army.
Standing Joint Committee of Industrial Women's Organization.
Union of Jewish Women.
Wesleyan Methodist Church (Committee of Privileges).
Women's Co-operative Guild.
Women's Freedom League.
Women's Liberal Federation.
Women's International League.
Women's Institute.
Women's Local Government Society.
Women's Municipal Party.
Young Women's Christian Association.

39.

Hundreds of societies hold a joint protest meeting against Regulation 40D in November 1918. The meeting wants Regulation 40D to be withdrawn because of the double sexual standards. Protests fail and the regulation is enforced until the end of the war. *HO 45/10893/359931* stands for everything that suffragists and feminists have been fighting against for over 50 years., and the WFL is quick to lead the opposition against it. It holds several mass meetings, with free admission to encourage a wider audience, in protest of the regulation which 'encourages state regulation of vice.' Further to this, they meet with parliament, who are also unhappy with the introduction of the act, albeit for differing reasons; parliament is upset that the act was passed without their consent as opposed to its content. Nonetheless, they raise the women's grievances in parliament. The WFL's protests are in vain and the regulation is upheld.

The WSPU also continue to hold rallies and mass meetings, but now they rally behind the government, not against them. Their new newspaper, Britannia, replacing The Suffragette, is fervently pro-war. They urge young men to do their duty and enlist into the military and for women to volunteer in munitions factories. Not all members of the WSPU are happy with this swift U-turn in policy however; many do not believe their national duty should be at the expense of the suffrage campaign, and the WSPU is beginning to fracture.

Even Sylvia Pankhurst is unhappy with the stance of her mother and sister, Christabel. Following in her father's steps, Sylvia has adopted increasingly staunch socialist views over the years and is discontented that the WSPU have focused their efforts too much on the recruitment of middle and upper classes. This, she believes, is to the detriment of the working classes. By 1913, she frequently addresses large crowds in the WSPU branches in the East End of London – a notorious hotspot of working-class communities - which are hugely important in recruiting hundreds more working-class women to the WSPU cause. Given these successes, various East End branches of the WSPU amalgamate under the new East London Federation of Suffragettes (ELFS), with Sylvia as the natural leader.

Sylvia focuses more of her energy on the ELFS after war breaks out. In contrast to her mother's orders to WSPU members, Sylvia urges her members to protest the war – fearing that the war will only bring hardship to the working classes. Sylvia is formally ousted from the WSPU.

As the war drags on, the government is aware that a reform of the current electoral procedure is needed. They know that they cannot have a situation where men who have fought for their country return home and can have no say in the running of the state.

As a new Representation of the People's Bill is being discussed in parliament in early 1917, which will give the vote to all men over the age of 21 years, Millicent Fawcett is working tirelessly for the government to include women in this Bill. Women, after all, are also playing their part for the country, she argues. Partly in recognition for the contribution being made by women, but due partly of fear for a militant resurgence in an already war-weary nation, the government agrees to extend the franchise to women. However, it applies only to women over the age of 30 who are property owners or married to property owners;

[8 GEO. 5.]   *Representation of the People Act*, 1918.   [CH. **64**.]

is not inhabited by the person in whose service A.D. 1918.
he is in such office, service, or employment, be
deemed to occupy the dwelling-house as a tenant;
and

(ii) for the purposes of this section the word tenant shall
include a person who occupies a room or rooms
as a lodger only where such room or rooms are
let to him in an unfurnished state.

4.—(1) A woman shall be entitled to be registered as a Franchises
parliamentary elector for a constituency (other than a university (women).
constituency) if she—

(*a*) has attained the age of thirty years; and

(*b*) is not subject to any legal incapacity; and

(*c*) is entitled to be registered as a local government elector
in respect of the occupation in that constituency of
land or premises (not being a dwelling-house) of a
yearly value of not less than five pounds or of a
dwelling-house, or is the wife of a husband entitled
to be so registered.

(2) A woman shall be entitled to be registered as a parliamentary elector for a university constituency if she has attained
the age of thirty years and either would be entitled to be so
registered if she were a man, or has been admitted to and
passed the final examination, and kept under the conditions
required of women by the university the period of residence,
necessary for a man to obtain a degree at any university forming,
or forming part of, a university constituency which did not at
the time the examination was passed admit women to degrees.

(3) A woman shall be entitled to be registered as a local
government elector for any local government electoral area—

(*a*) where she would be entitled to be so registered if she
were a man; and

(*b*) where she is the wife of a man who is entitled to be so
registered in respect of premises in which they both
reside, and she has attained the age of thirty years
and is not subject to any legal incapacity.

For the purpose of this provision, a naval or
military voter who is registered in respect of a residence qualification which he would have had but
for his service, shall be deemed to be resident in
accordance with the qualification.

A 2   3

In 1918, clause 4 is added to the Representation of the People Act. This gives the vote to women over 30 and are property owners, or have a university degree. In December 1918, for the first time ever, six million women are able to vote. *C 65/6385* or those who have a degree or carried out equivalent study at university. After much debate, the Bill is passed in parliament with an overwhelming majority on 6 February 1918; Asquith, too, in a U-turn of opinion, votes in favour of the Bill.

The women's suffrage societies know this does not go far enough to achieve what they have been fighting for: female suffrage to be on equal terms to male suffrage (the Bill has just extended the vote to all men over the age of 21). Demonstrations are held, but Millicent Fawcett and other women's suffrage leaders know that it would be far riskier to refuse the terms and demand full equality, which may be rejected with women making no gains at all. They accept the compromise for the considerable progress it achieves for female suffrage.

In December 1918, a month after the signing of the armistice that signalled the end of the Great War, the first peace-time General Election. Although many men have not yet returned home from the Front, for the first time ever, an extra 8.4 million women are able to vote. Christabel Pankhurst even stands as an MP but is pipped to the seat by the Labour Candidate, John Davidson. Although the wartime coalition government, led by Lloyd-George of the Liberal party, win, Constance Markiewicz, a woman, also wins a parliamentary seat. As, as a Sinn Fein representative, who has been fighting against the British Home Rule in Ireland, she declines to accept her seat at Westminster.

Nonetheless, after fifty years, this represents a huge victory.

CONCLUSION

NEW FEMINISM AND LEGACY

Despite the extension made to an extra six million additional women, women's suffrage movements could only claim a partial victory. The fight for equality continued.

Once the war was over, and demobilised soldiers began arriving home, the country sought a quick return to normality. The government thanked women for their contribution to the war effort, but, once the war had ended, most women were expected to leave their jobs for the returning veterans. Married women were amongst the first to be dismissed; with the return of their husbands – their dependents - the government, the press and the returning soldiers believed women had no reason to be financially independent. Women who refused were villainised. As a result, fewer women were employed in 1921 than in 1911.

Even the more practical shorter skirts and trousers were replaced with longer skirts and dresses once more. The country was desperate for a return to the pre-war ideals and values.

Any illusions that women had made permanent gains in society were soon dashed.

The NUWSS became the National Union of Societies for Equal Citizenship (NUSEC), and Millicent Fawcett gave way to Eleanor Rathbone as leader of the new women's society. The NUSEC continued the fight for women's equality, and broadened the campaign to include equality in many legal professions previously closed to women, equal pay and fairer divorce laws. However, there was a key difference to the pre-war campaign led by the NUWSS. NUSEC placed an emphasis on seeking reform and equalities for women primarily as mothers and wives; they fundamentally believed that women and men were different and that equality on exactly the same terms as men was impossible. A 'new feminism' emerged. This 'new feminism' angered those who sacrificed so much to achieve full equality with men. Millicent Fawcett retired altogether in 1926. The movement split.

The WSPU, which had become the Women's Party in 1917 as it shifted focus from women's suffrage to enlisting support for the war effort, also disintegrated. When Christabel Pankhurst, standing for the Women's Party, was defeated at the election in December 1918, the Women's Party rapidly lost ground until it finally crumbled in 1919.

The Pankhurst family, so prominent before the war in the struggle for women's suffrage, never united and the family rift remained. Christabel moved to California in 1921 bitterly believing that everything the WSPU had fought for would never be fully accomplished. Sylvia became ever more vocal as a communist sympathiser, and Adela remained in Australia after being banished by her mother for her opposition to militancy. She never saw her mother again.

Without any natural leadership, the suffrage societies after the First World War never emerged as strong, as united, or as imposing as its predecessors. They remained periphery groups, and the urgency and intensity of the pre-war tactics was never regained.

However, ten years after the end of the war, parliament was set to vote on an Equal Franchise Bill that would enable women to vote on the same terms as men. Key members of women's suffrage societies were invited to attend parliament to witness the final vote. Millicent Fawcett (NUWSS), Charlotte Despard (WFL), and Emmeline and Frederick Pethwick- Lawrence (WSPU) were there to witness the occasion. Emmeline Pankhurst died just weeks before the vote. It was passed by an overwhelming majority.

Suffragists had fought for fifty years to reach this point. There had been highs and lows, protests and violence. Many had sacrificed their freedom, health and, occasionally, their lives for the cause. As the 1920s drew to a close, some women, known as 'flappers', were beginning to realise the initial feminist vision of an independent woman; they felt empowered to drink in pubs, smoke in public and wear shorter hair and dresses. And, on 6 July 1928, they achieved the ultimate empowerment; equal suffrage was finally achieved.